NEW SAINTS AND BLESSEDS
OF THE CATHOLIC CHURCH

Volume 1

Pope John Paul II

FERDINAND HOLBÖCK

NEW SAINTS AND BLESSEDS OF THE CATHOLIC CHURCH

Blesseds and Saints
Canonized by Pope John Paul II
During the Years 1979–1983

Volume 1

Translated by
Michael J. Miller, M.Phil.

IGNATIUS PRESS   SAN FRANCISCO

Title of the German original
Neue Heilige der Katholischen Kirche
© 1991 Christiana-Verlag, Stein am Rhein

Cover photographs:
Upper left: Riccardo Filippo [Pampuri]
Upper right: Jacques-Désiré Laval
Lower left: Mary Anne Sala
Lower right: Maria Gabriella Sagheddu

Photos courtesy of
Photo-Archiv IMAGO SANCTORUM, Christiana-Verlag

Cover design by Riz Boncan Marsella

CONTENTS

SAINTS

Canonized by Pope John Paul II in the years 1979–1983

THE POPE AND HIS SAINTS

Beatification and canonization ceremonies are among the most solemn official acts of a pope—particularly because they are, in the opinion of many theologians, an expression of papal infallibility. As is well known, they are always preceded by a thorough and rigorously conducted juridical process of beatification or canonization, which must be successfully concluded. The process begins with the investigation by the diocesan bishop and then goes to the Sacred Congregation of Rites or, since 1968, to the Congregation for the Causes of Saints, where an Apostolic Process is conducted by several judges, a canon lawyer, and high-ranking members of a committee, who are to judge the life and death, the writings and works of the deceased person, and the authenticity of the miracles said to have been worked by God through the intercession of the person in question.

It has been considered until now the special glory of a pontificate when a pope, during his reign, could set before the faithful in the Church the greatest possible number of remarkable blesseds and saints as intercessors and examples, approving them for public veneration.

In this respect the first ten years of the present Pontiff's reign already far surpass the pontificates of his predecessors, for Pope John Paul II performed during those ten years ninety solemn ceremonies of beatification and twelve canonizations. In doing so, he departed—for the first time in several centuries—from the tradition that beatifications and canonizations be performed only in Rome. On quite a few occasions Pope John Paul II has carried out such solemn official acts at the most important stops on his apostolic journeys, whereby he has impressively demonstrated that the Church is a worldwide Church and that Christ "has purchased for God men of every race and tongue, of every people and nation" (cf. Rev 5:9).

It is too bad, though, that, of all the many blesseds and saints from diverse nations and languages, of various ages and occupations, whom John Paul II has raised to the honors of the altar, so few of them—there are exceptions—have become well known. This should be remedied by this first volume and its sequels, in which the blesseds and the saints whom Pope John Paul II has raised to the honors of the altar during the years of his pontificate are portrayed. The biographical sketch of each blessed or saint is followed by the homily, either in its entirety or somewhat abridged, that the Pope gave at the respective ceremony. In this way it can be demonstrated very impressively that these glorified brothers and sisters were truly "companions of ours in the human condition", as the Second Vatican Council has aptly expressed it in *Lumen gentium*, no. 50, and that they can show us "a most safe path by which, despite the vicissitudes of the world, and in keeping with the state of life and condition proper to each one of us, we will be able to arrive at perfect union with Christ, that is, holiness".[1]

May these short biographies show the people of our time that the Church, so often criticized today for the failings of her members, nevertheless has proved and still proves herself to be holy and the Mother of many holy ones.

Salzburg, the Solemnity of the Epiphany 1991
Ferdinand Holböck

---

[1] The papal homilies are reprinted, some in excerpt form, from *L'Osservatore romano* (English edition) or from the *Acta Apostolicae Sedis*.—TRANS.

BLESSEDS

Beatified by Pope John Paul II in the years 1979–1983

Alas, that I so late have known Thee,
Thou, above all, the loveliest,
Ah, that I did not sooner own Thee,
Thou greatest good and final rest!
It grieves me, I am sore reproved
That I so late have loved.
But I was blind and went astray,
I sought and sought and was not sated;
From Thee, alas, I turned away
To love the things Thou hast created.
I want to love Thee, O my Lord,
I want to love Thee, O my crown,
To love Thee, yea, without reward
Though in dire need I be cast down;
Fair Light, I'll love Thee for Thy sake
Until my heart shall break!

Angelus Silesius (1624–1677)
German poet

Blessed
Jacques-Désiré Laval

Doctor, Priest, Missionary

b. September 18, 1803, Croth
*d. September 9, 1864, on the Island of
  Mauritius*

Beatified April 29, 1979

A doctor who later became a priest and a missionary with extraordinary zeal for souls was beatified on April 29, 1979, by Pope John Paul II in Saint Peter's Basilica in Rome: Jacques-Désiré Laval,[1] who was born on September 18, 1803, in Croth, diocese of Évreux (France). After completing primary and secondary school, he studied at the Stanislaus College in Paris and earned a doctorate in medicine. He practiced then as a physician first in Saint-André-de-l'Eure and after that in Ivry-la-Bataille. He soon realized, though, that in the Church's difficult period of reconstruction in France after the Revolution of 1789 he would be able to accomplish more as a priest. He set out on June 15, 1835, once again for Paris, going this time to the seminary of the Sulpicians to study theology. On December 2, 1838, Laval was ordained a priest and immediately thereafter worked for two years as curate in Pinterville in Normandy. In 1841 the Jewish convert priest Francis Mary Paul Libermann (d. February 2, 1852), the venerable founder of the

---

[1] R. Piacentini, *Le Père Claver de l'Île de Mauritius* (Isodoun, 1949).

missionary Society of the Sacred Heart of Mary, which in 1848 was united with the Congregation of the Holy Spirit (the Spiritans), won him over for the missions among the natives of Africa and sent him to the island of Mauritius.

Jacques-Désiré Laval landed on September 14, 1841, in Port-Louis and immediately began missionary work with remarkable success among the black slaves who had been liberated in 1835 and 1839. By the time of his death on September 9, 1864, he had baptized fifteen thousand adults and converted approximately sixty-seven thousand black people. He has rightly been honored with the titles "Apostle of Mauritius" and "Peter Claver of the Island of Mauritius". While cholera epidemics raged on Mauritius in the years 1854, 1857, and 1862, the self-sacrificing priest lovingly attended to the sick and the dying in the hospitals he had constructed.

Through his exemplary life of prayer and extreme poverty, through his selfless devotion to the poor, whom he unfailingly treated with profound respect, by training and educating native catechists, pastoral counselors, and small Christian communities—which at that time was unheard of—and by organizing insurance and assistance programs, Father Laval transformed the entire island of Mauritius. "We see in Father Laval not the Roman Catholic priest but the saint who has done so much for the liberation of the Mauritians", said the head of the government, Dr. S. Ramgoolam, a Hindu, a man whose ancestors had come from that subcontinent of Asia where the sensibility for gurus and sadus, for holy men and leaders, is so pronounced.

Father Jacques-Désiré Laval died on September 9, 1864, having lived for twenty-three years on the island of Mauritius a life of prayer, labor, and suffering. His funeral turned into a triumphant procession; forty thousand people accompanied him to his final resting place. Men quarreled for the chance to carry the coffin for at least a few steps.

Much of what Father Laval said and did bears, of course, the stamp of the previous century; yet quite a lot of what has been started in the Church throughout the world only after and as a result of the Second Vatican Council was already being put into practice by him on the island of Mauritius: catechesis that is close to everyday life, a sharing of responsibility with the laity, small faith communities, worldwide Christian solidarity. "The Church of the poor" and "opening the doors" were for him, not worn-out slogans, but rather a service performed day in and day out. "Emancipation" meant to him more than mere economic advancement and recognition by society; it should be perfected in a freedom that embraces the entire person. His "conversion" in his younger years recalls Ignatius of Loyola; his humility, Francis of Assisi; his life of penance and prayer as well as his success in converting others, the Curé of Ars.

Pope John Paul II paid to this new blessed upon his beatification the following tribute:

> It is plainly impossible to point out here all the outstanding events in the life of Father Jacques-Désiré Laval, or all the Christian virtues that he practised to a heroic degree. Let us remember at least what characterizes this missionary, with regard to the mission of the Church today.
>
> It was in the first place his concern to evangelize the poor, the poorest, and, in this case, his "dear Blacks" of the island of Mauritius, as he used to call them. A Frenchman, he had begun by practising medicine in a little town in his native diocese, Évreux, but gradually the call to an undivided love of the Lord, which he had repressed for a certain time, made him abandon his profession and worldly life. "Once I am a priest, I will be able to do more good," he explained to his brother.
>
> A late vocation at St. Sulpice Seminary in Paris, he was at once put in charge of service of the poor; then, as parish priest of the little Norman parish of Pinterville, he shared all he had with those in want. But on learning of the misery of the Blacks of Africa and the urgency of bringing them to Christ, he obtained permission to leave for the island of Mauritius, with the Vicar Apostolic, Mons. Collier. For twenty-three years, until

his death, he dedicated all his time, used all his strength, and gave his whole heart to the evangelization of the inhabitants: indefatigably, he listened to them, catechized them, and made them discover their Christian vocation. He often intervened also to improve their medical and social condition.

His tenaciousness is an unending source of astonishment for us, especially in the discouraging conditions of his mission. But, in his apostolate, he always went to what is essential.

The fact is that our missionary left behind him innumerable converts, with a firm faith and piety. He was not given to sensational ceremonies, fascinating for these simple souls but with no lasting effect, or to flights of oratory. His educational concern was closely integrated in life. He was not afraid to return continually to the essential points of Christian doctrine and practice, and he admitted to baptism or to first communion only people prepared in little groups and tested. He took great care to put at the disposal of the faithful little chapels scattered over the island. Another remarkable initiative which links up with the concern of many pastors today: he had recourse to collaborators, [lay] men and women, as leaders of prayer, catechists, people who visited and advised the sick, others in charge of little Christian communities, in other words poor people, evangelizers of the poor.

What was, then, the secret of his missionary zeal? We find it in his holiness: in the gift of his whole person to Jesus Christ, inseparable from his tender love of men, especially the most humble among them, to whom he wished to give access to the salvation of Christ. Whatever time was not dedicated to the direct apostolate, he spent in prayer, especially before the Blessed Sacrament, and he continually combined with prayer mortifications and acts of penance which deeply impressed his confreres, in spite of his discretion and his humility.

He himself often expressed regret for his spiritual lukewarmness—let us say rather the feeling of his aridity; is it not precisely that he set the greatest store by fervent love of God and

Mary, to which he wished to initiate his faithful? That was also the secret of his apostolic patience: "It is on God alone and on the protection of the Blessed Virgin that we depend" (Letter of 6 July 1853). What a magnificent confession! His missionary spirituality had been, from the beginning, in keeping with the general pattern of a young Religious and Marian Institute, and he was always anxious to follow its spiritual requirements, in spite of his solitude and geographical distance: the Society of the Sacred Heart of Mary, of which he was one of the first members alongside the famous Father Libermann, and which was soon to merge with the Congregation of the Holy Spirit. The apostle, now as in the past, must in the first place maintain spiritual vigour within himself; he bears witness that he is continually drawing from the Source.

That is a model for evangelizers today. May he inspire missionaries and, I venture to say, all priests, who have in the first place, the sublime mission of proclaiming Jesus Christ and training the Christian life!

May he be, in a special way, the joy and stimulus of all religious of the Holy Spirit, who have never stopped implanting the Church, particularly in the land of Africa, and are at work there so generously!

May the example of Father Laval encourage all of those who, in the African continent and elsewhere, are endeavouring to build a brotherly world, free of racial prejudices! May Blessed Laval be also the pride, the ideal and the protector of the Christian community of the island of Mauritius, so dynamic today, and of all Mauritians![2]

[2] Homily during the beatification ceremony of Father Jacques Laval, C.S.Sp., and Father Francis Coll, O.P., *L'Osservatore romano*, May 7, 1979, p. 7.

Blessed
Francis Coll

Dominican

b. May 18, 1812, Gombreny
d. April 2, 1875, Vich

Beatified April 29, 1979

A Dominican who, after completing his formation in the order, was never able to live in a friary of his order but nevertheless gained for the Order of Preachers in the past [nineteenth] century the highest honor, the Spaniard Francis Coll[1] was elevated by Pope John Paul II on April 29, 1979, to the honors of the altar. The youngest of the twelve children of Pedro Coll Portell, a laborer in a wool-weaving mill, and Magdalena Guitart Anglada, he was born on May 18, 1812, in Gombreny, diocese of Gerona (Spain). After attending elementary school in his hometown, he entered the minor seminary in Vich to study humanities for four years and philosophy for three years (1823–1830).

On October 6, 1828, he began his novitiate with the Dominicans in Gerona, where he subsequently received minor orders, the subdiaconate, and was ordained a deacon (1833–1835). The peaceful life devoted to prayer and study was suddenly interrupted when a government decree of August 10, 1835, prohibited all religious orders in Spain, and, accordingly, the Dominicans of Gerona were

[1] Dominica de la Annunciata, *El Sueño de un Apostolo* (Barcelona, 1959); S. M. Bertucci, "Coll, Francesco", in *Bibliotheca sanctorum* 4:86–88.

forced to leave their friary. Francis Coll, however, was fortunate enough to be able to continue his theological studies at the major seminary in Vich and to complete them. There, on December 19, 1836, he was ordained to the priesthood.

For a short time the young priest worked at the Chapel of Saint George owned by the Puigallosas, a noble family, then in Artes, where he soon won the high esteem of the faithful. After that he was sent on a trial basis to Moyoa, a locality that had been torn apart by factions. Through the very first sermon he preached there, he succeeded in restoring peace to the area.

On the basis of his spiritual bond with the Dominican order, Francis Coll finally received permission from the bishop in authority to devote himself from then on exclusively to the preaching apostolate and to conduct days of recollection, spiritual exercises, and parish missions. So Father Coll for thirty years traveled on foot all over Catalonia. Throughout various dioceses, such as Barcelona, Lerida, Gerona, Vich, and Solsona, he was invited by pastors to preach and to give conferences, and everywhere he met with great success. Often the churches were too small to accommodate the multitudes that thronged to hear him, so many a time he had to move instead to the largest squares in the cities. Eventually people said: Wherever Father Coll comes to preach, morals improve and sinners convert, not because the preacher is so strict, but because he knows how to inspire confidence in the divine mercy. And his friend Saint Anthony Mary Claret used to say about Father Francis Coll: "In places where I have preached, Father Coll can still gather ears of wheat, but where he has preached, nothing is left over for me to do." Saint Anthony Mary Claret was also the one who obtained for Father Francis Coll from Pope Pius IX the honorific title of "Apostolic Preacher".

On November 6, 1850, Father Francis Coll was appointed the director of the Third Order Dominicans for all of Catalonia. In order to provide suitable instruction for girls, he founded on August 15, 1856, in Call-Nou in the diocese of Vich, the Congregation of Dominican Sisters of the Annunciation. This order of nuns developed very well under the direction of Father Francis Coll, who, over the course of eighteen years, from 1856 to 1874, served as ecclesiastical superior for this religious order of women. He composed for the members of this congregation several spiritual works, some of which saw many editions—for instance, *La hermosa rosa* (The beautiful rose), written in the Catalonian dialect (5th ed., 1912); then *La escala del cielo* (Ladder to heaven); and, most important, the rules of the order, the *Regla o forma de vivir de las Hermanas del Orden de Penitencia del padre san Domingo de Gutman* (3d ed., Valencia, 1956). This women's order today has 140 houses located throughout Europe and America and numbers more than two thousand Sisters.

Father Francis Coll, who was tall, well-mannered, and had a very impressive personality, suffered a series of strokes from December 2, 1869, on, which finally left him blind and very limited in his mental abilities. Nevertheless this Dominican, still living outside his community, continued to follow the rule of his order exactly. For he loved his order very much and was—in accordance with the stated purposes of his order—not only a great preacher but also a man greatly devoted to prayer.

On April 2, 1875, he died in Vich, and there, in the church of the motherhouse of the Dominican Sisters of the Annunciation, he was buried.

Pope John Paul II said about Father Francis Coll at the beatification ceremony on April 29, 1979:

> [Father Francis Coll:] a new glory of the great Dominican family and, equally so, of the diocesan family of Vich. A religious and at the same time a model apostle—for a large part of his life—in the ranks of the clergy of Vich.
>
> He was one of those ecclesial personalities who, in the second half of the nineteenth century, enriched the Church with new religious foundations; a son of Spain, of Catalonia, which has produced so many generous souls that have bequeathed a fruitful heritage to the Church.

In our case, this heritage took on concrete form in a magnificent and tireless work of evangelical preaching, which culminated in the foundation of the Institute known today as that of the Dominican Sisters of "La Anunciata". . . .

We cannot now present a complete portrait of the new Blessed, an admirable mirror—as you have been able to observe from a reading of his biography—of heroic human, Christian and religious virtues, which make him worthy of praise and of imitation in our earthly pilgrimage. Let us merely speak briefly about one of the most striking aspects of this ecclesial figure.

What impresses us most on approaching the life of the new Blessed is his evangelizing zeal. At a very difficult moment of history, in which social upheavals and laws persecuting the Church made him leave his convent and live permanently outside it, Father Coll, abstracting from human, sociological or political considerations, dedicated himself completely to an astonishing task of preaching. Both during his parish ministry, especially in Artés y Moya, and in his later phase as an apostolic missionary, Father Coll showed himself to be a true catechist, an evangelizer, in the best line of the Order of Preachers.

In his innumerable apostolic journeys over the whole of Catalonia, through memorable popular missions and other forms of preaching, Father Coll—Mosén [Moses] Coll, for many—was a transmitter of faith, a sower of hope, a preacher of love, peace and reconciliation among those whom passions, war and hatred keep divided. A real man of God, he lived fully his priestly and religious identity, made a source of inspiration in the whole of his task. To those who did not always understand the reasons for certain attitudes of his, he answered with a convinced "because I am a religious". This deep consciousness of himself was what directed his incessant labour.

An absorbing task, but which did not lack a solid foundation: frequent prayer, which was the driving power of his apostolic activity. On this point, the new Blessed spoke very eloquently. He himself was a man of prayer; he wished to introduce the faithful along this way (it is enough to see what he says in two publications of his, *La hermosa rosa* and *La escala del cielo*). It is the path he points out in the Rule to his daughters, with stirring words, which because of their relevance today I also make my own: "The life of Sisters must be a life of prayer. . . . For this reason I urge you over and over again, beloved Sisters: do not abandon prayer."

The new Blessed recommends various forms of prayer to sustain apostolic activity. But there is one that he prefers and which I have particular pleasure in mentioning and emphasizing: prayer while contemplating the mysteries of the Rosary: that "ladder to go up to heaven", composed of mental and vocal prayer which "are the two wings that Mary's Rosary offers Christian souls." A form of prayer which the Pope, too, practises assiduously and in which he calls upon all of you to join.[2]

[2] Homily during the beatification ceremony of Father Jacques Laval, C.S.Sp., and Father Francis Coll, O.P., *L'Osservatore romano*, May 7, 1979, p. 7.

Blessed [Saint] Henry de Ossó y Cervelló

Priest, Founder of a
Religious Order

b. October 16, 1840, Vinebre
d. January 27, 1896, Gilet

Beatified October 14, 1979
[*Canonized June 16, 1993*]

At the beatification ceremony on October 14, 1979, in Saint Peter's Basilica in Rome, presided over by Pope John Paul II, one of the most important Spanish personages of the last quarter of the nineteenth century, who promoted the reawakening of religious and ecclesiastical life in Spain, was raised to the honors of the altar: Henry de Ossó y Cervelló.[1]

He was born on October 16, 1840, in Vinebre, a small village in the province of Tarragona (diocese of Tortosa), the son of Jacob Ossó and Michaela Cervelló. His father wanted to make a merchant out of him, while his mother wanted him to be a priest. He received some commercial training from a brother of his father in Quinto de Ebro, near Saragossa. On September 15, 1854, his mother fell victim to a cholera epidemic; before she died she obtained from her son Henry the promise that he would become a priest. A few weeks later the fourteen-year-old Henry fled in secret to the Marian shrine on the mountain of Montserrat, to lead

[1] M. Gonzalez, *Don Enrique Ossó, o la fuerza del sacerdocio* (Barcelona, 1953); J. Fernandez Alonso, "Ossó y Cervelló", in *Bibliotheca sanctorum* 9:1288–90.

there the life of a hermit. When his relatives sought him, he returned home on the condition that they would let him become a priest. His father then gave his consent. Henry studied in Tortosa and Barcelona and on September 28, 1867, was ordained a priest. He celebrated his first Mass on October 6, 1867, the feast of the Holy Rosary, in Montserrat.

The young priest began his apostolate with an uncommon zeal for souls. Indeed, he was assigned to teach mathematics and physics at the seminary in Tortosa. This did not prevent him, however, from engaging first and foremost in catechetical activity and developing into one of the greatest teachers of religion in Spain. He wrote in 1872 the catechetical work *Guía práctica del Catequista en la enseñanza metódica y constante de la Doctrina Cristiana* (The Catechist's practical guide to methodical and faithful instruction in Christian doctrine). He devoted much time to the Catholic press, also, in order to counteract the anti-Christian and anticlerical tendencies of the day in Spain. In 1870 he founded and served as editor for the weekly *El amigo del Pueblo* and published the journal *Revista Teresiana* (Teresian Review), which found a large readership throughout Spain. In this journal the pious priest poured out his heart, so to speak, for even before his ordination he had been profoundly influenced by Saint Teresa of Jesus and her teaching about the spiritual life. For this reason he modeled his own spiritual life and his ministry upon that of the Saint of Avila. In 1873 he founded a Teresian Confraternity, whose members were required to spend fifteen minutes daily in contemplative prayer. For them he published in 1874 a valuable aid to contemplative prayer under the title *El cuarto de hora de oración* (The quarter of an hour of prayer), a little volume that has gone through forty editions—already more than fifteen by the time of the author's death.

The truly great work that Henry de Ossó then accomplished in the spirit of Saint Teresa of Jesus was the founding of the Society of Saint Teresa of Jesus, a congregation of Sisters dedicated principally to the education of children. Membership in the community today comprises two thousand nuns in fifteen countries. Henry de

Ossó founded still other apostolic societies, which in Spain during his lifetime numbered 130,000 members.

This saintly Spanish priest excelled in combining his extraordinary missionary activity with an intense life of contemplative prayer. In everything his concern was to further the interests of Jesus Christ. To this end he composed still other books and shorter works on the topics of spirituality, piety, religious pedagogy and catechetics, and even on Christian social teaching. He especially promoted the popularization of the social encyclical *Rerum novarum*, by Pope Leo XIII. Another of his special interests was promoting the revival of cloistered orders, which had been suppressed or dissolved by earlier Spanish regimes. Thus Henry de Ossó founded in Tortosa a cloister of Discalced Carmelite nuns and devoted his special love to the Abbey of Montserrat.

This noble, zealous priest died quite unexpectedly at the age of only fifty-five on January 27, 1896, in the Sanctus Spiritus Franciscan friary in Gilet, near Valencia, to which he had retreated for a time of recollection.

Pope John Paul II devoted to Blessed Henry de Ossó y Cervelló on October 14, 1979, a long homily, the essential parts of which are repeated here:

> Blessed Henry de Ossó offers us a living image of the faithful priest, persevering, humble and courageous in the presence of contradictions, completely disinterested, full of apostolic zeal for the glory of God and the salvation of souls, active in the apostolate, and contemplative in his extraordinary life of prayer.
>
> The period in which it fell to his lot to live was not an easy one, in a Spain divided by the civil wars of the nineteenth century and troubled by secularist and anticlerical movements in pursuit of political and social change, even giving rise to bloody revolutionary episodes. He, however, succeeded in remaining firm and intrepid in his faith, in which he found inspiration and strength to project the light of his priesthood upon the society of his time. He was clearly aware of what was his specific mission

as a man of the Church, which he loved deeply, without ever seeking leading roles in fields that were alien to his condition, and being open to everyone without distinction, in order to improve them and bring them to Christ. He carried out his resolution: "I will always belong to Jesus, as his minister, his apostle, his missionary of peace and love."

His priestly life, which lasted barely thirty years, gave rise to a continual development of apostolic enterprises, well pondered and carried out with abnegation, with impressive trust in God.

His was an existence of continual prayer which nourished his interior life and informed all his works. In the school of the great Saint of Avila, he learned that prayer, that "relationship of friendship" with God, is a necessary means to know oneself and live in truth, to grow in awareness of being sons of God, to grow in love. It is also an effective means to change the world. Therefore he was also an apostle and teacher of prayer. How many souls he taught to pray with his work *Cuarto de hora de oración* ([The] quarter of an hour of prayer)!

This was the secret of his great priestly life, which gave him joy, balance and fortitude; which made him—priest, servant and minister of all, suffering with all, loving and respecting all—feel happy to be what he was, aware that he had in his hands gifts received from the Lord for the redemption of the world, gifts which he, lowly and unworthy though he was, offered from the infinite superiority of the mystery of Christ and which filled his soul with ineffable joy. . . .

If we wish to point out now one of the most characteristic features of the apostolic nature of the new Blessed, we can say that he was one of the greatest catechists in the nineteenth century. . . .

As a brilliant catechist, he distinguished himself through his writings and through his practical work, taking care to make the *content of faith* known, adequately and in harmony with the Magisterium of the Church, and to help people to put it into practice in their lives. His active methods made him a forerun-

ner of later pedagogical discoveries. But above all, the aim he set himself was to make known and awaken love of God, of Christ and of the Church, which is the centre of the true catechist's mission.

In this mission he was familiar with all fields: that of childhood, with his unforgettable catechesis in Tortosa ("through the children to the hearts of men"); that of youth, with the Associations of young people, which spread far and wide; that of the family, with his religious propaganda writings, especially the *Teresian Review*; that of the workers, endeavouring to make them acquainted with the social doctrine of the Church; that of education and culture, in which, in conformity with the mentality of the age, he struggled to ensure the presence of the Catholic ideal in schools, at all levels, including universities. He dedicated himself tirelessly to the ministry of the spoken word, through preaching, and of the written word, through the press as a means of apostolate.

But in his catechetical effort, his favourite work, the one that took up most of his energies, was the foundation of the Society of St. Teresa of Jesus.

To extend the range of his action in time and in space, to penetrate into the heart of the family, to serve society in an age in which cultural formation was beginning to be indispensable, he enlisted the aid of women who could help him in this mission and dedicated himself to the task of forming them carefully. With them the new Institute began. It was to be distinguished by the following features: as daughters of their time, esteem for the values of culture; as women consecrated to God, their complete commitment to the service of the Church; as their specific style of spirituality, assimilation of the doctrine and example of St. Teresa of Jesus.

We could say that the Society of St. Teresa of Jesus was and is, as it were, the great catechesis organized by the Blessed Ossó in order to reach woman, and through her to instil new vitality in society and in the Church. . . .

For the Christian of today, plunged into an atmosphere of accelerated pursuit of a new ideal of man, the Blessed Henry de Ossó, the Christian educator, also leaves a heritage. This new man who is being sought cannot be truly such without Christ, the Redeemer of man. It will be necessary to improve him, educate him and ennoble him more and more in his multiple human aspects, but it is also necessary to catechize him, open him up to spiritual and religious horizons where he finds his dimension of eternity, as son of God and citizen of a world which goes beyond the present one. . . .

I pray to God that the Catholic tradition of the Spanish nation, of which the new Blessed spoke and wrote so much, may be a stimulus in the present phase of its history and that it may expand to include higher aims, looking decidedly to the future, but without forgetting, nay more, endeavouring to preserve and give new vitality to the essential Christian features of the past, in order that in this way the present may be an age of peace, material and spiritual prosperity, and hope in Christ the Saviour.[2]

---

[2] John Paul II, "Consistent Testimony of Faith in a Brilliant Catechesis", homily at beatification of Henry de Ossó y Cervelló, *L'Osservatore romano*, October 22, 1979, pp. 13–14.

Blessed
Joseph de Anchieta

Jesuit Missionary

b. *March 19, 1534, San Cristobal
de la Laguna*
d. *June 9, 1597, Iritiba*

Beatified June 22, 1980

On June 22, 1980, Pope John Paul II beatified the Jesuit Joseph de Anchieta,[1] that indefatigable and brilliantly gifted missionary whom Brazilians already revered as their national saint and as the "Apostle of Brazil".

This blessed was born on March 19, 1534, in San Cristobal de la Laguna on the island of Tenerife. At the age of fourteen he went to the Portuguese University of Coimbra. As a young student he heard the Lord instructing him to read the letters that his contemporary Francis Xavier (who was twenty-eight years his senior) wrote from his mission territory in the Far East to his superior, Ignatius of Loyola. This reading was probably one factor in Joseph's decision, at the age of seventeen, to enter the Society of Jesus. Kneeling before the miraculous image of the Blessed Virgin Mary in the Cathedral of Coimbra, he made a vow of celibacy and resolved to dedicate himself completely to the service of God. In

[1] E. Dominian, *Apostle of Brazil: The Biography of P. José de Anchieta SJ* (New York, 1958); C. Testore, "Anchieta, Giuseppe", in *Bibliotheca sanctorum* 1:1085–87.

1553, soon after he entered the order, the young Jesuit scholastic was sent to Brazil, where the Jesuits in 1549 had begun their missionary activity under Manoel de Nobrega. Anchieta worked first as an instructor at the school in S. Salvador de Bahia and then in the south of Brazil, particularly in the present-day states of São Paolo and Rio de Janeiro. He founded the College of São Paolo and served as its rector. The College of São Paolo, together with the Jesuit community and the order's province by the same name, developed on such a grand scale that the city, which today has over a million inhabitants, and the Brazilian state of São Paolo were named after it. In 1566 Anchieta was ordained a priest. In 1567 he accompanied the provincial superior Nobrega and helped him to found Rio de Janeiro. After this he was made superior of the Mission of São Vicente, which he governed until 1577, working primarily for the conversion of the Tapuyas Indians. Then from 1578 on he was provincial superior in Bahia. After 1591 Anchieta, prematurely aged and exhausted, lived in the Brazilian state that today is called Espirito Santo. In the village of Iritiba he died on June 9, 1597, renowned for his sanctity.

As an apostle to the Indians, Joseph de Anchieta became a legendary figure. Even before he was ordained a priest he had often accompanied the missionaries on their expeditions among the Indians. During those journeys he was twice in imminent danger of becoming the victim of cannibals. His charming personality and multilingual eloquence won the hearts of the savages, who followed Anchieta with a religious devotion. When the Huguenots under the command of Villegaignon took up a position on the Bay of Rio de Janeiro, it was due mainly to the influence of Joseph de Anchieta with the Tamoyos Indians that the intruders were not able to stand their ground. In the year 1563 a violent Indian uprising threatened to destroy the Portuguese. It was Anchieta, in union with Nobrega, who negotiated peace and risked his life for months by going over as a hostage to the insurgents in Iperoya. From the year of his priestly ordination on, Anchieta lived entirely for the mission among the Tupi and Guarani Indians. Robert Southey writes in his *History of Brasil*: "Barefoot, with his mission cross and rosary around his neck, his walking stick and Breviary in his hand, his shoulders loaded down with his Mass kit, José Anchieta advanced into the interior of the rainforest, swam across streams, clambered up uncharted mountainsides, was lost then in the depths of the wilderness, encountered ferocious beasts, and all of these toils and labors, which God alone witnessed, he carried out for one reason only: to win souls."[2]

The name of Blessed Joseph de Anchieta stands not only at the head of the history of missionary work in Brazil but also at the head of Brazilian cultural history. He was the first scholar and man of letters in the land; he was an unusually prolific author for the causes of education and the apostolate. He composed Latin dramas and dialogues made comprehensible to the natives by interludes in an Indian language. The most important of his literary works is a hymn of praise to Mary[3] in 2,086 couplets, which he drafted in 1563 while a prisoner of the savage Tamoyos Indians and wrote down on the sand of the seashore, then learned by heart, and finally set down on paper.

For the research historian, Anchieta's colorful missionary reports and private correspondence are of great significance. Eduardo Periè in his literary history of Brazil[4] calls Joseph de Anchieta the "true founder of Brazilian literature" (*verdadeiro fundador da Literatura brasileira*). In the field of linguistics, too, Anchieta was a pioneer. With a marvelous facility he mastered the Indian languages of southern Brazil and wrote the oldest grammar for the language of the Tupi Indians. A dictionary followed, and then poems and two catechetical works that are excellent, both for their erudition and for their precise knowledge of the indigenous language.

Pope John Paul II, in his homily at the beatification of Joseph de Anchieta, commended him by accentuating the following:

[2] Robert Southey, *History of Brasil*, in L. Koch, *Jesuitenlexikon*, vol. 2, col. 59, pp. 310ff.

[3] *Em Lovor da Virgem, poema em versos latinos* (Lisbon, 1672).

[4] Eduardo Periè, *Literatura brasileira nos tempos colonies*.

He loved with immense affection his brothers, the "Brasis", he took part in their life, studied their customs and realized that their conversion to the Christian faith would have to be prepared, helped and consolidated by an appropriate work of civilization, for their human advancement. His ardent zeal impelled him to carry out innumerable journeys, covering immense distances, in the midst of great dangers. But continual prayer, constant mortification, fervent charity, fatherly goodness, deep union with God, filial devotion to the Blessed Virgin—whose praises he sang in a long poem of elegant Latin verses—gave this great son of St. Ignatius superhuman strength, especially when he had to defend his native brothers against the injustices of the colonizers. He drew up a catechism for them, adapted to their mentality, which contributed greatly to their Christianization. For all this he well deserved the title of "Apostle of Brazil".[5]

---

[5] "Missionary Spirit of the Church Incarnated in New Blesseds, Pope John Paul's Homily on Sunday, June 22, 1980", *L'Osservatore romano*, June 30, 1980, pp. 10–11.

Blessed Mary of the Incarnation (Guyart)

Missionary Sister, Mystic

b. October 28, 1599, Tours
d. April 30, 1672, Quebec

Beatified June 22, 1980

In the first ten years of his pontificate, Pope John Paul II beatified several personages who meritoriously served the Church in Canada during her founding and development. Among them is the remarkable French mystic and missionary Sister of the Ursuline order, Sister Mary of the Incarnation (Marie Guyart).[1]

She was born on October 28, 1599, in Tours in western France, the fourth of eight children of Florentius Guyart and Jeanne (née Michelet), who worked as bakers. Even as a child she was very much predisposed to contemplative life. Her first vision was granted to her at the age of eight in the year 1607. At the age of fourteen she sensed an interior call to the religious life. She had to give in, though, to the demands of her father, who gave his eighteen-year-old daughter's hand in marriage to Claude Martin, a silk manufacturer. The marriage was happy, but it lasted only two years, as Claude Martin died in October 1619. From this marriage was born a son, Claude Martin, who became an exemplary and learned

---

[1] Marie of the Incarnation, *The Autobiography of Venerable Marie of the Incarnation*, trans. J. J. Sullivan (Chicago, 1964).

Benedictine monk in the Maurist Congregation, wrote the biography of his mother, and published her letters as well as her mystical writings.

The young widow refused the proposal of a second marriage. For almost ten years she helped out in the transport business of her brother-in-law Paul Buisson, taking a managerial position. In spite of her demanding duties in this business amid rough carriage drivers and enterprising merchants, Claude Martin's widow led during the years 1619 to 1631 an uninterrupted life of prayer in which she received mystical graces in ecstasies and visions. Marie Guyart-Martin made a vow of perpetual chastity and celibacy in 1621, and she added to that in 1624–1625 vows of poverty and of obedience as well. This total dedication of herself to God was rewarded on May 19, 1625, with a first vision of the Trinity, which was followed by a profound insight into the mystery of the Incarnation of the Son of God, whereby she saw Jesus take her heart and bind it intimately with his own. In 1627 a second vision of the Trinity was accorded to this thoroughly devoted woman, an even greater blessing than the first. At that time the resolve matured in this highly favored soul to consecrate herself to God in the religious life.

On January 21, 1631, Marie Guyart-Martin entered the Ursuline community in Tours, accompanied as far as the convent gate by her thirteen-year-old son, Claude, whom she, in obedience to the Lord, entrusted to her relatives for his further education. Two months after she entered the religious order, God granted her a third trinitarian vision, in which she was brought into mystical communication with the three Divine Persons. Strangely enough, this pinnacle of mystical union was followed immediately by great darkness and dryness in the spiritual life, so that—united with Christ, who suffered external and internal abandonment upon the Cross—her soul might attain genuine fruitfulness in missionary activity.

In fact, Sister Mary of the Incarnation (Marie de l'Incarnation)—her name since entering religion—then experienced more and more urgently the feeling that she absolutely had to go forth into the missions to save souls. It became clear to her at that time that she was called quite specifically to the missions in Canada, even though it seemed impossible to carry that out.

In a meeting with Madame de la Peltrie, from Alençon, in February 1639, Sister Mary of the Incarnation immediately recognized that this woman was the lady she had seen in a prophetic dream who had demanded that she move to Canada to undertake missionary work there. She glimpsed then also what she would encounter in Canada: "An endless cross, interior abandonment by both God and creatures to a degree that was truly crucifying, and with that a life of complete obscurity." And so it was, too.

Blessed Mother Mary of the Incarnation, first superior of the Ursuline Sisters in Canada (New France). After spending thirty years in the world, two of them as a married woman, while leading a life of prayer and penance, she labored with all her strength for thirty-three years in Canada for the conversion of the Indians. She died on the last day of April in the year 1672 at the age of seventy-two.

On February 22, 1639, Sister Mary of the Incarnation, accompanied by young Sister Mary of Saint Joseph, left the cloister in Tours and traveled to Paris, where during a two-month stay everything necessary to found a convent in Canada was arranged. On May 4, 1639, Sister Mary of the Incarnation, together with three Augustinian nursing Sisters, boarded the ship *Saint Joseph*, which set sail for Canada. On August 1, 1639, she went ashore at Cape Diamond and settled in the city of Quebec, where she founded her first Ursuline community. From this outpost she became the very soul of the Canadian missions. People seeking counsel and assistance came to her more and more often in ever greater numbers. In the midst of trials and afflictions caused by war, earthquakes, floods, and fires, Sister Mary of the Incarnation attended to everyone. She was for all who came to her not only the superior of the convent but also a kind and helpful mother, who gave her whole heart to the native Indians in order to win them for Christ. She learned their dialects so well that she was able to compose dictionaries for the various Indian languages and even catechisms to go with them. With unceasing prayer this zealous Ursuline nun accepted the penances and sacrifices that were imposed on her by God or by her fellow men or which she demanded of herself in her untiring missionary work.

On April 30, 1672, Mary of the Incarnation died in the odor of sanctity. Pope John Paul II called this Ursuline nun, whom he beatified on June 22, 1980, "Mother of the Catholic Church in Canada" and spoke of her as follows:

Her catechetical apostolate on behalf of the natives is indefatigable: she composes a catechism in the language of the Hurons, another in the language of the Iroquois, a third in the language of the Algonquins.

A deeply contemplative soul engaged, however, in apostolic action, she makes a vow to "seek the greatest glory of God in everything that would be of greatest sanctification", and in May 1653, she offers herself interiorly as a sacrifice to God for the good of Canada.

A teacher of the spiritual life, to the extent that Bossuet defined her [as] the "Teresa of the New World", and a promoter of works of evangelization, Mary of the Incarnation united contemplation and action admirably in herself. In her, Christian woman was fulfilled completely and with unusual balance, in her various states of life: wife, mother, widow, business woman, religious, mystic and missionary, and all that in faithfulness to Christ, always in close union with God.[2]

Convent of the Ursuline Sisters in Quebec, which was built after 1640 by Mary of the Incarnation. The Indian tents in the foreground are meant to show that the Indians entrusted their daughters to Sister Mary of the Incarnation.

[2] *L'Osservatore romano,* June 30, 1980, pp. 10–11.

Blessed
Peter de Betancur

Religious Brother

b. May 16, 1619, Villaflor
d. April 25, 1667, Guatemala

Beatified June 22, 1980

In Villaflor on the island of Tenerife this blessed, who would help the Church in Latin America to flourish, was born on May 16, 1619, as the fifth and last child of a family descended from the Norman conqueror of the Canary Islands, Juan Betancur. Peter de Betancur[1] spent all of his childhood and adolescence as a shepherd. Yet even during this time the pious youth disciplined himself and fasted four times a week on bread and water—a practice that he continued until the end of his life.

After mature consideration Peter deliberately passed up an opportunity to marry a suitable bride, and on September 18, 1649, at the age of thirty, he boarded a ship that sailed for South America. In Havana, where he disembarked, he felt like a complete stranger in the hubbub of this great colonial city. He was just waiting for a chance to travel farther to Honduras, and meanwhile he made use

[1] A. Martinez Cuesta, "Betancur", in *Dizionario degli Istituti de perfezione*, vol. 1, cols. 1412–15; D. Vela, *El hermano Pedro en la vida y en las letras* (Guatemala, 1935); F. Vásquez de Herera, *Vida y virtudes del venerable Pedro de San José Betancur* (Guatemala, 1962).

of the time by learning the weaving trade in the wool-weaving mill of a certain Jerome Suarez. On February 18, 1651, after a very strenuous voyage, Peter arrived in Guatemala with a high fever, which forced him to remain there for a while. He was admitted to the royal hospital in the city for treatment. Thus he became acquainted with the world of the sick and suffering, to which he thereafter confined his efforts until the end of his life, knowing that he could accomplish much good among the sick. After Peter's discharge from the hospital, Captain Antonio Lorenzo, who likewise was a descendant of the Betancur family, took him into his own household, where the servant and squire brought Peter into contact with the church circles in the city. Peter sensed an interior call to become a priest, but he had neither the aptitude nor the money needed for study.

During Lent Peter took up work in the great wool-weaving mill of Petrus d'Armengol. He befriended a son of his employer, who was a student. The latter wanted to teach Peter reading, writing, and the fundamentals of literacy. He had very little success at this, however. After two years of laborious effort, Peter had scarcely succeeded in grasping and committing to memory the basic elements of grammar. Nevertheless, the young student presented to his Jesuit teachers his awkward and uneducated pupil with the request that they take him into their care. They did in fact accept him into their grammar school. Peter made every effort he could to learn, but again he made only meager progress. At the end of the year 1654, he was forced to give up his studies and to renounce his dream of becoming a priest. But during this time two things had taken root quite firmly in his mind and heart, namely, the counsels of the *Imitation of Christ* and the catechism of the saintly Doctor of the Church Robert Bellarmine. He took the *Imitation of Christ* seriously through an extraordinarily severe ascetical life; at night he scourged himself and spent hours in contemplation of the life of Jesus. At this time also Peter began his custom of walking through the streets of Guatemala at night, wearing a hair shirt and carrying a heavy cross on his shoulders.

On January 14, 1655, Peter received from the hands of his confessor, the Franciscan Father Fernando Espino, the habit of a Franciscan tertiary. He was fully determined now to lead a life of strict self-denial, fasting, and praying, consecrated to God in the authentic spirit of Saint Francis of Assisi. Brother Peter spent some time in the hermitage of El Calvario in the vicinity of Guatemala City. With his brothers in the Third Order he rebuilt this hermitage into a large church.

Until 1658 Peter divided his time between prayer, work, and serving as watchman at the newly constructed church. Eventually an ever-increasing number of tertiaries followed his example. Peter succeeded in starting the custom of a weekly Rosary procession on Saturday through the streets of Guatemala. On these processions he observed that poverty and need were to be found in houses throughout the city. He began to take care of all those who were poor, sick, or in need. Peter did not hesitate to knock at the doors of the rich to beg alms for his "patients". He soon noticed, though, that this form of charitable activity would always remain insufficient unless he institutionalized it at a fixed location. To this end he obtained, with the alms he had collected, the modest dwelling of an old woman who had died. This house was gradually transformed into a "Bethlehem", where he took children in off the streets, to care for them and to instruct them, and where he also sheltered the homeless, including sick people who had been released from the hospital before they were completely cured. At the center of this shelter, which kept growing larger with new additions, was a statue of Our Lady of Bethlehem. Peter's co-workers, headed by his friend and assistant Antonio de la Cruz, formed a confraternity, the Bethlehemites (*Belemitas*), under his direction and at first lived according to the Third Order rule of Saint Francis.

The spirituality of Brother Peter was plain and simple, in keeping with the artlessness of a peasant. It was love in particular that inspired all of his work and prayer, sacrifice and atonement for the sake of the poor and the sick. Then came three other important virtues, namely, deep humility, a spirit of penance, as well as ardent prayerfulness. With moving humility he cared for the despised black slaves and for those people who lived on the margins of society.

In humility he persevered in his nocturnal walks through the city streets carrying a heavy cross on his shoulders. Now and then his naïveté drove him to ridiculous lengths in his ascetical practices; when he met with mockery or scorn on this account or when people played insulting jokes on him, this did not affect him in the least. Brother Peter fled from all comfort and convenience. He mortified himself in a heroic manner, with respect to food and clothing and even in his sleep. For fourteen years no one ever observed him using a bed, for he would sleep leaning against a wall or on the floor with his hands under his head. He fasted four times a week, and in the final years of his life a meal for him consisted only of a gruel into which he put the bread crumbs left over from the hospital. Throughout his life Betancur was an almost terribly strict ascetic, who, nevertheless, spontaneously and happily sang Marian hymns and would dance before the Christmas crib. Prayer was the constant driving force of his life. He contemplated over and over again the mystery of the triune God dwelling in the soul of the person in a state of grace; then he would repeat incessantly the Our Father and the Hail Mary of the Rosary. He had an especially intimate devotion to the Blessed Virgin Mary and to the Poor Souls in Purgatory.

Brother Peter de Betancur died a rich man, with regard to his merits, on April 25, 1667. Pope John Paul II beatified Brother Peter de Betancur and raised him to the honors of the altar on June 22, 1980, together with four other worthy personages in the history of Christendom in North and South America: Mary of the Incarnation, Francis de Montmorency-Laval, Joseph de Anchieta, and Kateri Tekakwitha. Thus the litany of the blesseds and saints in the New World was happily lengthened.

His community of Bethlehemites for the care of the sick and the instruction of poor children spread to Mexico, Peru, and the Canary Islands. Members of the community lived by the rule of the Franciscan Third Order and according to the instruction that

Brother Peter had written for his first co-worker, Brother Antonio de la Cruz.[2] In addition he left also a Testament[3] and a collection of prayers.[4] The Confraternity received ecclesiastical approval on May 2, 1667, a few days after the founder's death. Pope Clement X ratified their Constitutions in 1672, Pope Innocent XI in 1687 gave permission to confraternity members to take solemn vows, and Clement XI granted them in 1707 the privileges of mendicant orders and clerics regular.

During the beatification ceremony at Saint Peter's Basilica in Rome on June 22, 1980, Pope John Paul II summarized the life of Peter de Betancur thus:

Peter de Betancur came from the Canary Islands. He was born on March 21, 1626, in Villaflor on Tenerife to a poor family. Already as a child he had to get used to heavy work on the farm. His close contact with nature, though, directed his thoughts to God and led him to develop a deep prayer life and great trust in Divine Providence. Gradually a desire awakened in him to become a herald of the Gospel. At the age of thirty he sailed for the New World. For seventeen months his arduous travels lasted, until finally, on February 18, 1651, having arrived in Guatemala, he exclaimed: "Here I want to live and die!"

He became first and foremost a friend of the poor and of children. He taught them the catechism and instructed them in the rudiments of reading and writing. His spirituality was that of Saint Francis of Assisi and therefore he joined the Third Order Franciscans. Increasingly he devoted himself to the poor. His straw hut, the "little house of Our Lady of Bethlehem", became a charitable center. Peter de Betancur became the founder of a confraternity devoted to the care of the sick and to

---

[2] Pedro Betancur, "Instrucción al hermano Antonio de la Cruz", *Reglas de la confraternidad de los Betlemitas.*

[3] Betancur, *Testamento auténtico del venerable hermano Pedro de San José Betancur.*

[4] Betancur, *Memorias de las coronas que han rezado los hermanos y devotos de la Virgen Nuestra Señora en Guatemala los años 1661 y 1666.*

schoolteaching, which today, as the Congregation of the Bethlehemites, has spread to Mexico, Peru, and the Canary Islands. Betancur died on April 25, 1667, in Guatemala.[5]

[5] The English edition of *L'Osservatore romano* of June 30, 1980, p. 10, gives the following summary, which is different from the one cited by Professor Holböck:

Born of a poor family, engaged in farming and cattle rearing, Peter de Betancur has only one aim in his life: to bring the Christian message to the "West Indies". At the age of 23 he leaves his country and arrives at Guatemala, sick, without resources, alone, unknown. He becomes the apostle of negro slaves, of the Indios subjected to inhuman labour, of the emigrants, without work or security, of abandoned children. Brother Peter, inspired by the charity of Christ, became everything for everyone, in particular for little vagabonds of any race and colour, for whom he founds a school. For poor sick people, discharged from hospital but still in need of help and assistance, Peter founds the first hospital in the world for convalescents. He died at the age of 41.

The Child of Bethlehem, in whose name he founded the Bethlehemite Congregation, was the assiduous subject of the spiritual meditation of the Blessed, who was always able to see in the poor the face of "the Child Jesus": for this reason he loved them with delicate tenderness, the memory of which is still alive in Guatemala.

(The *Acta apostolicae sedis*, in its reprint of John Paul II's homily [July 31, 1980] and of the decree of beatification [May 2, 1981], gives his date of birth as March 21, 1626; his age at traveling to the New World as twenty-three; and his age at death as forty-one. The confusion may have arisen from baptismal records. In the Betancur family there may have been a cousin, also named Pedro, who was born in 1619. The later, "official" birthdate makes more plausible the plans of the blessed at various stages of his life.—Trans.)

Blessed Francis de Montmorency-Laval

Bishop

b. April 30, 1623, Montigny-sur-Avre

d. May 6, 1708, Quebec

Beatified June 22, 1980

Two hundred seventy-two years after his death in Quebec, the first bishop of this Canadian city was beatified on June 22, 1980, and raised to the honors of the altar. He earned this honor, no doubt, as a pioneer of the kingdom of God in the New World both as a priest and as a bishop who was acutely aware of Jesus' great commission, "Go out into the whole world. . . ."

Francis de Montmorency-Laval[1] was born on April 30, 1623, in Montigny-sur-Avre (Eure). His wish to become a priest was fulfilled in 1647, when he received priestly orders. In 1649 he was appointed archdeacon of Évreux. As such he participated in founding the seminary of the Paris Foreign Missions. In 1653 he was appointed apostolic vicar for Tonkin in Indochina. It was not possible for him, however, to assume this post in the Far East. Alexander VII in the year 1658 appointed Francis de Montmorency-Laval apostolic vicar for New France, which meant for the French colonies in America (Canada).

---

[1] A. Mulders, *Missionsgeschichte* (Regensburg, 1960), p. 345; A. Gosselin, *F. Montmorency-Laval, premier évêque de Québec* (Quebec, 1944).

After being consecrated titular bishop of Petra, he landed on March 16, 1659, in his mission territory in the New World and then zealously began a tireless campaign to awaken the faith of the white settlers and to win the natives to Christianity and to instruct them in it. For this purpose he erected a series of parishes and developed in this regard quite a marvelous pastoral ministry. Besides this he actively contributed to the material welfare also of this French colony, energetically fought against the exploitation of the natives, opposed the sale of alcohol to the Indians, and fearlessly contested the Gallican claims of several of the king's civil appointees. He obtained from King Louis XIV many privileges for the Church in Canada, such as the erection of the diocese of Quebec, of which he was appointed the first bishop in October 1674. He founded in Quebec a major seminary with a theological faculty, which in 1852 became Laval Catholic University, named after him. The seminary where he lived was not only the place for the education of future priests but also the fatherhouse for the clergy who were aged or infirm. The clergy had their center of gravity in the seminary, as the bishop wanted it to be. Therefore not only the income of the local parishes but usually the personal funds of the priests as well were made over to the seminary, which then took care of the shared financial burdens equitably.

In the year 1668 Bishop Montmorency-Laval had to step down for reasons of health. He retired to the seminary in Quebec that he had founded, where he spent his days praying and making many sacrifices for his diocese and its advancement, until on May 6, 1708, he was called to his eternal reward.

Blessed Francis de Montmorency-Laval devoted the greater part of his episcopal ministry to missionary journeys and the visitation of parishes in his immense diocese of Quebec, which in those days extended from Canada to the Gulf of Mexico. He visited the missionaries at their lonely stations and encouraged them to persevere; he preached the gospel to his dearly beloved Indians and administered the sacraments to them thousands of times; with all this he did not forget the three thousand French colonists who had settled in between the regions inhabited by the Indians. Through his foundations—above all the first seminary in North America and many parishes—he made a decisive contribution to the future of religion on the North American continent. For "the diocese of Quebec and its seminary, which was affiliated with the seminary of the Paris Foreign Missions, remained during the eighteenth century the center of evangelization in Canada and far beyond it."

At the beatification of Bishop Francis de Montmorency-Laval on June 22, 1980, Pope John Paul II said:

> Francis de Montmorency-Laval, a noble son of France, also animated by missionary charism, could have aspired to the most promising human careers, but he preferred to respond generously to the invitation of Christ, who sent him to proclaim the Gospel in distant countries. Elected Vicar Apostolic in "New France", invested with the episcopal character, he settled in Quebec and dedicated himself with indefatigable zeal to the expansion of the Kingdom of God, realizing in himself the ideal figure of the bishop. He devoted to the Indians the primary part of his ministry. He traveled incessantly throughout the immense region, half of the North American continent; he founded the seminary of Quebec, which would then become the "Laval University", one of the first Catholic universities of modern times. He devoted special care to priests, men and women religious; he obtained from the Holy See the institution of a seminary in Paris for the "Foreign Missions".
>
> Mary of the Incarnation, who had preceded him in Canada twenty years earlier and who is beatified with him today, wrote on his arrival: "He is a man of great merit and outstanding virtue; it is not men who have chosen him; I will say in all truth that he lives like a saint and like an apostle." [2]

[2] *L'Osservatore romano*, June 30, 1980, p. 11.

Blessed
Kateri Tekakwitha

Virgin

b. 1656, Ossernenon
d. April 17, 1680, Caughgnawaga,
  Quebec

Beatified June 22, 1980

The "Lily of the Mohawks",[1] as the first American Indian blessed of the United States and Canada has been called, was born in 1656 in Ossernenon near Auriesville, New York. Her father was a heathen Iroquois, her mother a Christian Algonquin. Both parents died during the smallpox epidemic in 1660, when Kateri was only four years old. She survived the horrendous epidemic and lived then with the family of an uncle, who was a heathen. The name Tekakwitha, which was given to her when she was a child, means "Puts Things in Order". It was not she, however, but God who put everything in order for her by arranging that she should learn about the Christian faith. Her respect for it increased, and she began to love Christ more and more. The French Jesuit Father Jacques de Lamberville administered to her at Easter in 1676 the Sacrament of Baptism and gave her the name Kateri (Catherine) as a sign of the virginal purity that she had maintained throughout her childhood and youth while living among pagans. Kateri's heathen uncle insisted that she should marry, and so she fled to the Saint Francis

[1] Franz Weiser, *Das Mädchen der Mohawks: Die selige Kateri Tekakwitha 1656–1680* (Stein am Rhein: Christiana-Verlag, 1987).

Xavier mission station, La Prairie de la Madeleine, near Montreal on the Saint Lawrence River. Here the young Christian woman gave an extraordinary example of deep spirituality and self-sacrificing devotion.

At Christmas 1677 Kateri received her First Holy Communion. Two years later, on March 25, 1679, she made a vow of perpetual virginity. From that day on she devoted herself even more to prayer and led a remarkably penitential life of exemplary holiness.

The first accounts of the life of young Kateri were handed down from generation to generation as part of the oral tradition of the Indians. Then in 1715 the missionary Father Gotonec wrote down the accounts of persons who had known Kateri personally. Among the things they noted: "Every day at four o'clock in the morning Kateri would go to church. . . . During the day she interrupted her work from time to time and spent the hours that she could spare in earnest prayer. In the evening she visited the church again and did not leave until the night was far advanced."

Prayer and work, then, made up Kateri's day. She tried to apply her faith, as she understood it, to everyday life in a radical way. She would have been happy to enter a religious order, but before she could take any concrete steps toward that goal she was called to her eternal reward, on April 17, 1680. She died, having precociously attained perfection. The story of her saintly life and death and her reputation continued to spread among the Indians. Many visited her grave in the "Village of Prayer" in Caughgnawaga. On June 22, 1980, Pope John Paul II beatified this American Indian woman.

The Austrian Jesuit Father Franz Weiser studied the history of the missions among the American Indians for years on location and then wrote a comprehensive biography of the fairest flower of those missions, Blessed Kateri Tekakwitha.

Pope John Paul II paid the young blessed the following tribute at her beatification:

This wonderful crown of new Blesseds, God's bountiful gift to his Church, is completed by the sweet, frail yet strong figure of a young woman who died when she was only twenty-four years old: Kateri Tekakwitha, the "Lily of the Mohawks", the Iroquois maiden who, in seventeenth-century North America, was the first to renew the marvels of sanctity of Saint Scholastica, Saint Gertrude, Saint Catherine of Siena, Saint Angela Merici and Saint Rose of Lima, preceding, along the path of Love, her great spiritual sister, Thérèse of the Child Jesus.

She spent her short life partly in what is now the State of New York and partly in Canada. She is a kind, gentle and hardworking person, spending her time working, praying and meditating. At the age of twenty she receives Baptism. Even when following her tribe in the hunting seasons, she continues her devotions, before a rough cross carved by herself in the forest. When her family urges her to marry, she replies very serenely and calmly that she has Jesus as her only spouse. This decision, in view of the social conditions of women in the Indian tribes at that time, exposes Kateri to the risk of living as an outcast and in poverty. It is a bold, unusual and prophetic gesture: on 25 March 1679, at the age of twenty-three, with the consent of her spiritual director, Kateri takes a vow of perpetual virginity—as far as we know the first time that this was done among the North American Indians.

The last months of her life are an ever clearer manifestation of her solid faith, straightforward humility, calm resignation and radiant joy, even in the midst of terrible sufferings. Her last words, simple and sublime, whispered at the moment of death, sum up, like a noble hymn, a life of purest charity: "Jesus, I love you. . . ." [2]

---

[2] *L'Osservatore romano*, June 30, 1980, p. 11.

Blessed
Mary Anne Sala

Religious

b. April 21, 1829, Brivio (Lecce)
d. November 24, 1891, Milan

Beatified October 26, 1980

During the process for the beatification of the Italian school Sister
Mary Anne Sala,[1] one decisive witness was the mother of Pope
Paul VI, Signora Giuditta Montini-Alghisi, who in her youth went
to a school run by the Marcelline Sisters and received instruction,
training, and Christian formation from one of them, namely, Sister
Mary Anne Sala, who impressed her deeply by her exemplary life
as a religious, her unstinting self-sacrifice, her piety, and her faith.

Mary Anne Sala, who was raised to the honors of the altar by
Pope John Paul II on October 26, 1980, was born the fourth of
eight children of well-to-do Christian parents on April 21, 1829, in
Brivio (Lecce) in northern Italy. Because of her outstanding intelligence, it was decided that the girl would have an education, and
in 1840 at the age of eleven she was sent to the boarding school of
the Marcelline Sisters in Vimercate, not far from Milan. Only two
years had passed since the good professor and spiritual director of
the major seminary in Milan, Monsignor Luigi Biraghi, with the

---

[1] A. Portaluppi, *Vita della Serva di Dio Maria Anna Sala delle Marcelline* (Milan, 1931);
Maria Ferragatta, *Visse per le anime: Un'educatrice modello* (Milan, 1963).

help of Sister Marina Videmari, had founded a community of Sisters in Cernusco sul Naviglio for the religious and moral education of the young women of the province of Milan, which he placed under the patronage of Saint Marcellina. This saint, who was born in the year 330 in Trier (Treves), the daughter of a Roman prefect and the sister of the Milanese bishop Saint Ambrose, consecrated herself to God by a vow of virginity and assisted in the education of her two brothers, Ambrose and Satyr, and so can serve indeed as an excellent example and a powerful intercessor for women religious who devote themselves to the instruction and training of youth.

Mary Anne Sala received an excellent education from these Marcelline Sisters. She acquired during this time not only a teacher's diploma but also, and most important, outstanding womanly virtues. In 1846 Mary Anne returned to the bosom of her family, where she was a comforting angel to her parents, who were in dire straits due to illness and financial difficulties, and where she became an apostolically minded helper for the children and the needy of the parish. Soon, though, Mary Anne sensed that Christ was calling her to consecrate herself to him completely and unreservedly in religious life. In 1848 she entered the community of the Marcelline Sisters in Vimercate. Her excellent character helped her to live up to the twofold demands that were made of the members of this newly founded religious congregation: to lead a very intense spiritual life and yet at the same time to work zealously in the apostolate of educating the young.

In the year 1852 Mary Anne Sala was among the first group of Marcelline Sisters to make perpetual vows. She was then assigned to teach primary school and music in Cernusco sul Naviglio, later in Genoa and Milan, where she was remarkable for her constant fidelity to the rule and for her unselfish, maternal care for her pupils, so that she earned the titles of the "Living Rule" (*la regula vivente*) and "Mother of Souls" (*madre delle anime*).

In 1878 she left Genoa, where she had worked diligently for nine years at a thoroughly successful apostolate, and came to Milan.

There she served with Sister Marina Videmari, the co-founder of the Congregation of Marcelline Sisters, as her assistant and also as a teacher in the higher grades of the school, and proved herself to be a devoted and exemplary school Sister, even when heroic obedience and exceptional Christian patience were demanded of her. In spite of a very painful tumor on her neck, she persevered in fulfilling her duties with undiminished alacrity and with perfection until her death on November 24, 1891.

Pope John Paul II in his homily at the beatification emphasized the following features of the life of this blessed:

Sister Mary Anne Sala teaches us heroic faithfulness to the particular charism of vocation.

Having entered the Marcelline Sisters at the age of twenty-one, she realized that her ideal and her mission should be solely teaching, education, the formation of girls at school and in families.

Sister Mary Anne was simply and entirely faithful to the fundamental charism of her Congregation. Three great lessons spring from her life and example: the necessity of formation and possession of a good character, firm, sensitive, well-balanced; the sanctifying value of commitment in the duty assigned by obedience; and the essential importance of teaching work.

Sister Mary Anne aimed at acquiring the virtue of ability in the highest degree, convinced that what one can give depends on what one possesses; and she took an enthusiastic interest in her task as a teacher, sanctifying herself in accomplishment of her daily work. She put into practice the message of Jesus: "He who is faithful in a very little is faithful also in much" (Lk 16:10). Let Sisters above all learn from the new Blessed to be joyful and generous in their work, even if it is hidden, monotonous, lowly! Let all those dedicated to educational work learn never to be frightened by the difficulties of the times, but to commit themselves with love, patience, and preparation in their mission, such an important one, of forming and elevating minds to the supreme transcendent values. Today particularly, the School needs educators who are wise, serious, qualified, sensitive, and responsible.[2]

---

[2] "A Priest, a Religious and a Layman Attest That All Are Called to Holiness", *L'Osservatore romano*, November 3, 1980, p. 10.

Blessed Bartolo Longo

Lawyer, Founder of New Pompei

b. February 11, 1841, Laziano (near Brindisi)
d. October 5, 1926, Pompei

Beatified October 26, 1980

By constantly praying the Rosary many saints have not only deepened their life of faith in a special way but have even attained perfection and holiness and merited eternal happiness in heaven. So it was in any case with the attorney Bartolo Longo,[1] who was beatified by Pope John Paul II at the end of the month of the Holy Rosary, October, in the year 1980.

Bartolo was born on February 11, 1841, in Laziano, near Brindisi in southern Italy, the son of Bartolomeo Longo and Antonia (née Luparelli). As a youngster, he received an education in the humanities, from 1846 to 1858, in the Royal Collegium Ferdinandeum of the Piarist Fathers in Francavilla Fontana. After a childhood and youth spent happily and virtuously, he studied law in Lecce and then, from 1863 on, in Naples. At the university there in those days a vociferously unchristian and anticlerical spirit prevailed. As a result, Bartolo Longo's faith was very badly shaken during the years he was a university student. Where faith has weakened, it often happens that superstition and then disbelief enter in. So it was with

---

[1] Ida Lüthold-Minder, *Die Rosenkranzkönigin von Pompei und ihr Advokat Bartolo Longo* (Hauteville, Switzerland, 1981).

the young law student Longo. From false friends he picked up an interest in spiritualism, which at that time in Naples had all but taken on the form of an institutionalized religion, with temples, rituals, ceremonies, and cultic attendants, drawing people into contact with demonic powers, almost along the lines of a satanic cult. Fortunately, Bartolo Longo had not allowed his friendly ties with one believer, a deeply spiritual professor by the name of Vincenzo Pepe, to break off. This man convinced the young law student to confide all his doubts and difficulties to a very highly educated, saintly Dominican priest, Father Radente. This priest succeeded in leading Bartolo Longo back to the faith, indeed, to the regular and fervent recitation of the Rosary.

After Bartolo Longo completed his study of law and obtained a doctorate on December 12, 1864, he returned to his family and began to practice as an attorney. Moreover, he was now living a life of pious faith and works of charity. Twice during this time he was close to getting married. He renounced those plans, however, on the basis of the prophetic words that the saintly Redemptorist Father Emanuel Ribera had spoken to him: "The Lord wants to do very great things through you. You are called to fulfill a very important mission."

Finally Bartolo Longo gave up his law practice. He went back to Naples to do apostolic and charitable work in the slums of this major city. In doing so he became acquainted with a wealthy young widow, the countess Marianna de Fusco. Bartolo Longo became administrator of the real estate of this countess as well as the tutor and governor of her children. He also accompanied her when she inspected her various properties. These journeys revealed to him the material poverty and the even greater religious and moral poverty of the small tenant farmers and laborers on the lands of Countess de Fusco. Bartolo Longo felt more and more strongly that help was absolutely needed there and that it should consist not only of socioeconomic improvements for these people but also and primarily of their liberation from religious ignorance and indifference. Bartolo Longo wanted to achieve this through the Rosary and to help these people, most of whom could not even read or write, by teaching them first of all to pray the Rosary correctly. Indeed, he was convinced that the Rosary would give these ignorant, uneducated people a basic understanding of the most important truths of salvation in the life of Jesus and Mary and would certainly make them, if only they would pray the Rosary constantly, not only more pious but also better off.

In the small, extremely humble, nearly dilapidated village church in the valley of Pompei, Bartolo Longo sought to gather the people and bring them back to the practice of the faith. At first he had almost no success at all. Then someone presented him with a picture of the Queen of the Holy Rosary that had been bought at a flea market in Naples. He placed this picture on the altar of the little village church. Then the "miracle" happened: more and more people came to pray devotedly and perseveringly before the Marian image. Suddenly prayers began to be answered and remarkable miracles started to take place through the intercession of the Queen of the Holy Rosary. News of this spread rapidly through the whole region. Finally, so many people were coming to pray before the picture of the Queen of the Holy Rosary that the church was too small for them and needed to be enlarged. Those who planned to enlarge the building would not be content with a "normal" village church; they planned to build for the Queen of the Holy Rosary a magnificent, artistically ornamented basilica. The driving force behind this was Bartolo Longo. He begged for the funds that would be needed and organized everything for love of his heavenly Mother. The former attorney devoted all of his talents, not only to the construction of the Rosary basilica in New Pompei and to the promotion of fervent recitation of the Rosary in the basilica as it took shape; he also founded and edited the magazine *Il Rosario e la Nuova Pompei*, and in it, as well as in numerous other publications, he defended by means of the written word the truths of salvation that the Rosary presents for meditation—truths that were then, as they still are today, being attacked, called into question, or openly denied and disputed.

Still, Bartolo Longo was not satisfied with promoting piety among the people and deepening their faith. He knew that, if faith is to be genuine, it simply has to manifest itself in good deeds done for one's neighbor. So next to the Rosary basilica in New Pompei he also constructed an orphanage for boys and girls and a large home for the children of criminal fathers and mothers who had been imprisoned. His trust in the Queen of the Holy Rosary never failed, even when failures and difficulties, lack of appreciation and misunderstandings occurred and hindered his apostolic and charitable projects. When good people misjudged him and his selfless efforts, when bad people scoffed at him or made him out to be a fraud or a thief who embezzled contributions or misused them to his own advantage, Blessed Bartolo Longo was undaunted and kept on working, even after the onset of illnesses and physical sufferings in his later years.

On May 30, 1925, when Bartolo Longo received from Cardinal Augusto Sili a special award for the great services he had rendered, he said,

Today, in the presence of distinguished personages and in the presence of my many adopted children, my dear orphans, I wish to make my last will and testament, since my final hour will soon arrive. I have collected sums of money in the millions and then spent them in order to construct the Rosary basilica and the large charitable institutions in this new city of Mary. I possess nothing now, for I have just given the entire work over to the Apostolic See. All that I have left are the awards that have been given to me. I leave them to my orphans, so as to remind them that one must be valiant as a knight in the practice of virtue, and strong and unshakable in faith. To Your Eminence, on the other hand, since you are the papal delegate and administrator of the basilica and of the works that I founded, I leave my feeble body with the request that it be buried in the sanctuary of the basilica at the foot of the throne of my gracious Queen, whom for over twenty years I have tried to serve faithfully.

In a little room within the orphanage beside the basilica, Bartolo Longo, this deeply devoted, faith-filled layman, who loved the Queen of the Rosary with all his heart, spent the last years of his life in almost uninterrupted prayer.

On October 5, 1926, on the eve of the feast of the Holy Rosary, Blessed Bartolo Longo died at the age of eighty-five, holding in his right hand a crucifix and in his left hand the rosary that had slipped through his fingers over and over again in unceasing prayer and through which he had accomplished so much for the honor of the Queen of the Holy Rosary.

At the beatification of Bartolo Longo on October 26, 1980, Pope John Paul II said the following about him:

> Bartolo Longo, the founder of the famous Sanctuary of Pompei, to which I went with deep devotion a year ago [in 1979]; he is the apostle of the Rosary, the layman who lived his ecclesial commitment completely.
>
> Bartolo Longo was the instrument of Providence for the defence and witness of Christian faith and for the exaltation of the Blessed Virgin in a painful period of scepticism and anti-clericalism.
>
> His long life, inspired by a simple and heroic faith and rich in inspiring episodes, in the course of which the miracle of Pompei sprang up and developed, is well known to everyone. Beginning with humble catechesis to the peasants of the Valley of Pompei, and the recitation of the Rosary before the famous picture of the Madonna, up to the erection of the stupendous Sanctuary and the institution of the works of charity for sons and daughters of prisoners, Bartolo Longo carried on with intrepid courage a magnificent work which leaves us amazed and lost in wonder even today.
>
> But above all, it is easy to note that his whole existence was an intense and constant service of the Church in the name of, and out of love for, Mary.
>
> Bartolo Longo, a Tertiary of the Dominican Order and

founder of the Institution of Sisters "Daughters of the Holy Rosary of Pompei", can really be defined "the man of the Madonna": out of love for Mary, he became a writer, an apostle of the Gospel, propagator of the Rosary and founder of the famous Sanctuary, in the midst of enormous difficulties and adversities; out of love for Mary, he created institutes of charity, went begging for the children of the poor, transformed Pompei into a living citadel of human and Christian goodness; out of love for Mary, he bore tribulations and calumnies in silence, passing through a long Gethsemane, always confident in Providence, always obedient to the Pope and to the Church.

With the Rosary in his hand, [he said on March 11, 1905, and] he says to us, too, Christians of the end of the twentieth century: "Reawaken your trust in the Blessed Virgin of the Rosary. . . . You must have the faith of Job! . . . Adored Holy Mother, I place in you every affliction of mine, all hope and all confidence!"[2]

Following the example of Blessed Bartolo Longo, the *Supplica* has become a custom in the Rosary basilica in New Pompei: twice a year, on the eighth of May and on the first Sunday in October, the month of the Holy Rosary, the faithful "storm heaven with prayers" confidently offered to the Queen of the Holy Rosary. This custom spread throughout Italy and beyond to the whole world. Pope John Paul II recalled this on May 8, 1983, in his Angelus address in the following words:

Today in the Pontifical Sanctuary of the Most Blessed Virgin of the Most Holy Rosary of Pompei, the centenary of the "Supplication" to Our Lady is being solemnly celebrated.

This fervent and heartfelt prayer, which is recited at noon every year on 8 May and on the first Sunday of October, flowed from the great heart of Blessed Bartolo Longo, the lawyer who

[2] "A Priest, a Religious and a Layman Attest That All Are Called to Holiness", *L'Osservatore romano*, November 3, 1980, pp. 10–11.

was born in Latiano (Brindisi) in 1841 and died in Pompei in 1926 after a long life dedicated to an intense and fruitful apostolate, especially in the field of the welfare and education of children, through splendid works of charity such as shelters, laboratories, schools, recreation centres, workshops, orphanages, built around the Sanctuary of Pompei, which he wanted to dedicate to the Most Holy Virgin of the Rosary.

The generosity of the faithful of all continents has made that Sanctuary ever more beautiful in recent years and has contributed to the vitality of the social initiatives intended by the Blessed for the authentic social and Christian development of children.

Divine Providence deigned to give me the joy of elevating Bartolo Longo to the glory of the altars on 26 October [1980] through beatification. And today, on the centenary of the "Supplication", I too wish to join the endless crowd gathered in fervent prayer in that Sanctuary of the Madonna, and in the great square of Pompei.

I therefore invite everyone who is listening to me at this moment to associate spiritually with this praying chorus and to follow the last part of the "Supplication", which I am now about to recite:

"O blessed Rosary of Mary, sweet chain that ties us to God, bond of love that unites us to the angels. Tower of salvation during the assaults of hell, safe port in the common shipwreck, we will never leave you again. You will be a comfort to us in the hour of agony, to you will be the last kiss of fading life. And the last utterance from our lips will be your sweet name, O Queen of the Rosary of Pompei, O dear Mother of ours, O Refuge of sinners, O consoling Sovereign of the sorrowful. May you be blessed everywhere, today and always, on earth and in heaven. Amen." [3]

[3] "Honouring Our Lady of the Rosary of Pompei", *L'Osservatore romano*, May 16, 1983, p. 2.

Blessed
Luigi Orione

Priest, Founder of Various
Congregations

b. June 23, 1872, Pontecurone
d. March 12, 1940, San Remo

Beatified October 26, 1980

"Apostle of charity, Father of the poor, outstanding benefactor of the afflicted"; by these titles Pope John Paul II called Don Orione, who was beatified on October 26, 1980, and they were certainly no exaggeration. Everything that this Italian priest undertook he did as a servant of the pope, the bishops, and the Church for the benefit of his fellow men in need.

Luigi Orione[1] was born on June 23, 1872, in Pontecurone (diocese of Tortona), son of the liberal-minded road worker Vittorio Orione and the intelligent, very pious Carolina (née Feltri). She raised her three children, especially her son Luigi, in an exemplary manner and was a valuable support to him in the early years of his apostolic work for children.

As the boy matured, so, quietly and interiorly, did his vocation to the clerical state; in September 1885, scarcely thirteen years old, he asked to be admitted to the Franciscans in Voghera and was accepted. Unfortunately, after one year a serious inflammation of

[1] G. Papasogli, *Vita de Don Orione* (Turin, 1975); A. Pronzato, *Don Orione, il folle di Dio* (Turin, 1980).

the lungs forced the young religious candidate to leave the friary. After he recuperated, he began to help his father in road construction work. He maintained later that this was for him a very useful time that gave him a genuine understanding of the plight and the needs of manual laborers.

Thanks to the concern of the local pastor, in whom the pious youth confided, he was able to go to Turin in September 1886 to study at the Oratory of Don Bosco; the saintly Salesian, then in the final years of his life, was Luigi's confessor and made a profound impression on the boy and on his subsequent life and work. On December 8, 1886, Don Bosco's successor, Blessed Don Rua, permitted the fourteen-year-old youth to take a vow of chastity.

In the year 1889 Orione entered the major seminary in Tortona, where he distinguished himself by his extraordinary zeal in striving for perfection and in apostolic work. In 1892 the ambitious candidate for the priesthood was allowed to assume the duties of custodian at the cathedral and to live alone in a garret over the cathedral. Here, following the example of Don Bosco, Orione began to gather children about him on Sundays and holy days. On July 3, 1892, with the approval of the bishop and of the seminary rector, the candidate for the priesthood started the Oratory of Saint Louis, the forerunner of the many great works that Luigi Orione would go on to found as a priest. In October 1893 he founded in the San Bernardino section of the city of Tortona a small residence for needy seminarians who were not housed in the seminary. While still a subdeacon, Orione received faculties from the bishop to preach throughout the diocese. On April 13, 1895, he was ordained a priest. From that moment on he bestowed all of the love of his priestly heart upon poor children, arranging and caring for their instruction in schools and for their recreation at summer camps (*colonie agricole*). In order to staff these summer camps properly, Don Orione founded the congregation of the Little Work of Divine Providence, for which he obtained the approbation of the local ordinary on March 21, 1903.

After the dreadful earthquake in Messina on the island of Sicily in December 1908, Don Orione hurried to the site to stand by the stricken people in their time of need and especially to gather to himself the children who had been orphaned so abruptly and to place them in homes. Pope Saint Pius X at that time made Don Orione the vicar general of the diocese of Messina for three years. Don Orione also helped with the relief efforts in 1915 after the earthquake in Marsica by caring for the orphaned children of that region.

In the education of the young, Don Orione found his inspiration in the methods of Saint John Bosco. For his charitable works, though, he followed closely the example of Saint Giuseppe Benedetto (Joseph Benedict) Cottolengo. He traveled back and forth through all of Italy with undiminished zeal to save souls, to awaken vocations to the priesthood and religious life, and to find helpers for his charitable works, which became ever more numerous. One after the other he founded religious congregations: the Sons of Divine Providence, the Little Missionary Sisters of Charity, and the Sacramentine Sisters. He sent his spiritual sons and daughters beyond the borders of Italy to Brazil and Argentina, founded houses in the United States, in Poland and in England, in Chile and Uruguay. Untiringly he organized popular missions and pilgrimages and in many locations set up charitable centers that he called "Piccolo Cottolengo".

When his confreres and doctors insisted that this indefatigable priest relax for a few days at the Villa Santa Clotilde in San Remo, it became evident that all of his physical strength was exhausted. He died quite unexpectedly on March 12, 1940, in San Remo, very much against his will, for he had explained shortly before that he wanted to die "not under palm trees, but in the midst of his poor people", whom he identified with Jesus Christ. On the day of his death, 820 religious belonged to his various religious congregations, of whom 220 were priests.

The remains of this marvelous priest, who had accomplished more than could ever be told, were carried in a triumphant funeral procession through many cities in northern Italy and then laid to rest in the crypt of the Marian shrine he had constructed, the Madonna della Guardia in Tortona. Twenty-five years later, in 1965, when the casket was opened to examine the remains, the entire body of Don Orione was found to be completely incorrupt.

"Don Luigi Orione appears to us as a marvellous and brilliant manifestation of Christian charity", said Pope John Paul II during the beatification ceremony in Saint Peter's Square in Rome. To these words he added the following sentences:

> It is impossible to summarize in a few sentences the adventurous and sometimes tragic life of the one who defined himself, humbly but wisely, as "God's porter". But we can say that he was certainly one of the most eminent personalities of this century, due to his Christian faith, professed openly, and his charity, lived heroically. He was, entirely and joyfully, the Priest of Christ, travelling all over Italy and Latin America, dedicating his life to those in greatest suffering from misfortune, want, and human wickedness. Let it be enough to recall his active presence among the victims of the earthquakes in Messina and Marsica. Poor among the poor, driven by love of Christ and brothers in greatest need, he founded the Little Work of Divine Providence, the Little Missionary Sisters of Charity, and later the Blind Sacramentine Sisters and the Hermits of St. Albert.
>
> He also opened other houses in Poland (1923), in the United States (1934), and in England (1936), in a real ecumenical spirit. He then wished to give his love for Mary concrete shape by erecting at Tortona the wonderful Sanctuary of Our Lady of Custody. It moves me to think that Don Orione always had a special predilection for Poland and suffered immensely when my dear country was invaded and torn apart in September 1939. I know that the Polish red and white flag, which he carried triumphantly in a procession to the Sanctuary of Our Lady in those tragic days, still hangs on the wall of his modest room in Tortona: he himself wanted it there! And in the last greeting he uttered in the evening of 8 March 1940, before going to San Remo, where

he was to die, he said again, "I love the Poles so much. I have loved them since my boyhood; I have always loved them. . . . Always cherish these brothers of yours."

From his life, so intense and dynamic, there emerge the secret and originality of Don Orione: he let himself be led only and always by the rigorous logic of love! Immense and complete love of God, Christ, Mary, the Church, the Pope, and equally absolute love for man, the whole of man, body and soul, and all men, little and great, rich and poor, humble and wise, holy and sinful, with special kindness and tenderness for the suffering, the underprivileged, the desperate. He enunciated his programme of action as follows: "Our policy is the great and divine charity which does good to all. Let our policy be that of the Our Father. We look at nothing else but souls to save. Souls and souls! That is our whole life; that is the cry and our programme; our whole soul, our whole heart!" And he exclaimed with lyrical tones: "Christ comes bearing on his heart the Church, and in his hand the tears and blood of the poor: the cause of the afflicted, the oppressed, widows, orphans, the lowly, outcasts; new heavens open up behind Christ: it is, as it were, the dawn of God's triumph!"

He had the character and the heart of the Apostle Paul, tender and sensitive to the point of tears, tireless and courageous to the point of daring, tenacious and dynamic to the point of heroism, facing dangers of every kind, approaching high personalities of politics and culture, illuminating men without faith, converting sinners, always immersed in continual and confident prayer, sometimes accompanied by terrible penances. A year before his death he had summed up as follows the essential programme of his life: "To suffer, be silent, pray, love, crucify oneself and worship." God is wonderful in his saints, and Don Orione remains a luminous example and comfort in faith for everyone.[2]

---

[2] *L'Osservatore romano*, November 3, 1980, p. 10.

Blessed [Saints] Lawrence Ruiz and His Fifteen Companions

Married Man, Sacristan

d. *August 14, 1633, Nagasaki*

Beatified February 18, 1981
[*Canonized October 18, 1987*]

This chapter is about those heroic witnesses[1] to the faith who were martyred during the years 1633 to 1637 in Nagasaki, Japan. They suffered martyrdom after the 205 heroes who shed their blood and died for the faith in the years 1617–1632 in Omura-Nagasaki and who were beatified in 1867 by Pope Pius IX.

This persecution of the Christians was started by the supreme commander of the Japanese armed forces, Tokugawa Yemitsu, on February 28, 1633, by an edict declaring that foreigners who preached Christianity and their Japanese accomplices in this perverse business would have to be detained in the prison at Omura. A new kind of punishment for the Christians was then introduced: "the gallows and the pit" (*anatsurushi*). The condemned person was stretched out and fastened to a wooden beam, then suspended and lowered to the waist into a vat filled with garbage. From 1634 on, those who professed the Christian faith were subjected to horrendous torture before their crucifixion.

[1] I. Venchi, "Ibáñez de Erquicia, Domenico", in *Bibliotheca sanctorum, Prima appendice* (Rome, 1987), pp. 665–67.

The sixteen martyrs belonged in varying degrees to the Holy Rosary Province of the Dominican order, also called the Philippine Province, which had been founded in 1587 for the evangelization of China and which had established a vice-province around the year 1600 in Japan.

The group of martyrs from the years 1633 to 1637 consists of nine priests, two lay brothers, two tertiaries, and three laymen.

The names of the martyrs are as follows:

1. Lawrence Ruiz: he was the father of a family from Manila who, as a member of the Rosary sodality, served the Dominicans as sacristan.

2. Domingo Ibáñez de Erquicia: he was born in 1589 in Guipúzcoa (Basque region, Spain), made his profession in the Dominican order in 1605, was sent to the Philippines in 1611, and was a missionary there in Luzon, then a professor at Saint Thomas College in Manila. Father Domingo worked in Japan from 1623 on; in 1628 he was made provincial vicar of the Dominican order in Japan.

3. Francisco Shoyemon: born in Japan, he was the guide of Father Domingo and a catechist. In prison he was admitted by Father Domingo into the Dominican order as a lay brother. He died on August 14, 1633.

4. Jacobo Kyushei Gorobioye Tomonaga: this Japanese native became a priest of the Dominican order in 1626 in Manila. From 1632 on he worked on Taiwan (Formosa) and then in his Japanese homeland.

5. Michael Kurobioye: the Japanese guide of Father Jacobo Kyushei, he was also a catechist. He died on August 17, 1633.

6. Lucas Alonso: he was a Spaniard, born in 1594 in Carracedo (Zamora, Spain). Starting in 1618 he was a missionary in the Philippines and a professor in Manila; for ten years he did mission work in Japan.

7. Matthaeus Kohioye: he was born in 1615 in Arima (Japan); he worked as a catechist at the side of Father Lucas Alonso, who during their imprisonment admitted him into the Dominican order as a lay brother. He died a martyr on October 19, 1633.

8. Magdalena of Nagasaki: she was born in 1610 and as a Dominican tertiary made a vow of perpetual virginity. She died on October 15, 1634.

9. Marina of Omura: this Japanese virgin was a member of the Dominican Third Order and showed exceptional hospitality to the missionaries. She was tortured over a slow fire and died on November 11, 1634.

10. Jordanus Hyacinth Ansalcone: he was born in 1689 in San Stefano Quisquina on the island of Sicily; from 1632 on he cared for the sick of the Chinese communities in Manila and in Japan.

11. Thomas Hioji Rokuzayemon Nishi: he was born in 1590 in Hirodo (Japan); he worked as a missionary on Taiwan (Formosa) and from 1629 on in his Japanese homeland. He died on November 17, 1634.

12. Antonio González: he was a Spaniard from León. He served as professor of theology and for a short time as rector at Saint Thomas College in Manila. He was then leader of the group of missionaries who went to Japan in 1636 to support the Christians there who had been deprived of their shepherds. He died in prison after repeated torture on September 24, 1637.

13. Michael de Aozaraza: he was born in 1598 in Onate (Guipúzcoa, Basque region, Spain); he became a priest and a missionary.

14. Vincent Shiwozuka: he was a Japanese priest who had fled to Manila.

15. Lazarus of Kyoto: he was a Japanese layman who had fled to Manila. Father Vincent Shiwozuka and Lazarus of Kyoto were cruelly tortured and then abandoned the Catholic faith for a short time; they soon reconsidered, were reconciled with God and with the Church, and went to a bloody death as martyrs on September 29, 1637.

16. Guillaume Courtet: he was a French Dominican priest.

At the beatification ceremony for the martyrs Lawrence Ruiz and his fifteen companions in Luneta Park in Manila on February 18, 1981, Pope John Paul II said:

The City of Manila and all the Philippines are filled with joy on this day as they sing a hymn of glory to Jesus Christ. For, according to his Gospel promise, Christ is truly acknowledging, in the presence of his Father in heaven, those faithful martyrs who acknowledged him before men (cf. Mt 10:32). And because of the nearness of Luneta Park to old Manila "intra muros", the hymn of glory to God which has just been sung by numberless voices is an echo of the Te Deum sung in the Church of Santo Domingo on the evening of 27 December 1637, when the news arrived of the martyrdom at Nagasaki of a group of six Christians. Among them were the head of the mission, Father Antonio González, a Spanish Dominican from León, and Lorenzo Ruiz, a married man with a family, born in Manila "extra muros" in the suburb of Binondo.

These witnesses had also in their turn sung psalms to the Lord of mercy and power, both while they were in prison and during their execution by the gallows and the pit, which lasted three days. The song of these "designated" martyrs—to use a definition made by my predecessor Benedict XIV—was followed in Manila, then as now, by the song of thanksgiving for the martyrs now "consummated" and "glorified". *Te martyrum candidatus laudat exercitus*: they belonged indeed to a white-robed throng, whose members included those of the white legion of the Order of Preachers. . . .

The sixteen blessed martyrs, by the exercise of their priesthood—that of Baptism or of Holy Orders—performed the greatest act of worship and love of God by the sacrifice of their blood united with Christ's own Sacrifice of the Cross. In this way they imitated Christ the priest and victim in the most perfect way possible for human creatures (cf. *S. Th.* II-II, q. 124, a. 3). It was at the same time an act of the greatest possible love for their brethren, for whose sake we are all called to sacrifice ourselves, following the example of the Son of God who sacrificed himself for us (cf. 1 Jn 3:16).

This is what Lorenzo Ruiz did. Guided by the Holy Spirit to

an unexpected goal after an adventurous journey, he told the court that he was a Christian, and must die for God, and would give his life for him a thousand times.

"*Kahit maging sanglibo man / Ang buhay n'yaring katawan / Pawa kong ipapapatay, / Kung inyong pagpipilitang / Si Kristo'y aking talikdan* (Even if this body would have a thousand lives / I would let all of them be killed / If you force me to turn my back to Christ)."

Here we have him summed up; here we have a description of his faith and the reason for his death. It was at this moment that this young father of a family professed and brought to completion the Christian catechesis that he had received in the Dominican Friars' school in Binondo: a catechesis that cannot be other than Christ-centred, by reason both of the mystery it contains and the fact that it is Christ who teaches through the lips of his messenger.

This is the Christian essence of the first Beatus of the Philippine nation, today exalted as a fitting climax to the fourth centenary of the Archdiocese of Manila. Just as the young Church in Jerusalem brought forth its first martyr for Christ in the person of the deacon Stephen, so the young Church in Manila, founded in 1579, brought forth its first martyr in the person of Lorenzo Ruiz, who had served in the parish church of Saint Gabriel in Binondo. The local parish and the family, the domestic church, are indeed the centre of faith that is lived, taught and witnessed to.

The example of Lorenzo Ruiz, the son of a Chinese father and Tagala mother, reminds us that everyone's life and the whole of one's life must be at Christ's disposal. . . . But the attractive figure of the first Filipino martyr would not be fully explained in its historical context without extolling the witness given by his fifteen companions, who suffered in 1633, 1634 and 1637. They form the group led by two men: Domingo Ibáñez de Erquicia, the vicar provincial of the Japanese mission and a native of Régil in the Spanish Diocese of San Sebastián; and Jacobo

Kyuhei [*sic*] Tomonaga, a native of Kyudetsu in the Diocese of Nagasaki. Both of these belonged to the Dominican Province of the Holy Rosary in the Philippines, established in 1587 for the evangelization of the Far East. The whole group of Lorenzo's companions was composed of nine priests, two professed brothers, two members of the Third Order, and a catechist and a guide-interpreter. Nine were Japanese, four were Spaniards, one a Frenchman, and one an Italian. They had one reason for their evangelical witness: the reason of Saint Paul, baptized by Ananias to carry the name of Christ to all peoples (cf. Acts 9:15): "We have come to Japan only to preach faith in God and to teach salvation to little ones and to the innocent and to all the rest of the people." Thus did the martyr Guillaume Courtet sum up their mission before the judges at Nagasaki. . . .

Four of the new Beati were professors in the College [of Saint Thomas in Manila], one was also the Rector, and a fifth had studied there. In the first century of the evangelization of the Far East, begun by the preaching of Saint Francis Xavier, the Philippine Islands had already, in this university institution, a further means of carrying out the mission of evangelization. A fruitful programme aimed at imparting theological knowledge and propagating the faith, which still today is enhanced by the cultural heritage of the Philippines and vivified by the Christian spirit, is a fitting instrument for assisting the spread of the Gospel.[2]

The martyrs of Nagasaki who were beatified on February 18, 1981, in Manila were canonized by Pope John Paul II on World Mission Sunday, October 18, 1987, in St. Peter's Square in Rome during sessions of the World Synod of Bishops dealing with the theme of "The Mission of the Laity in the Church". In his homily on that occasion the Pope emphasized, understandably, the missionary character of the Church and the duty of all members

---

[2] *L'Osservatore romano*, February 23, 1981, pp. 15–16.

of the Church, including the laity, to take seriously Christ's command to bring the Good News to all the world. Excerpts from the Pope's homily follow:

> These holy martyrs (of Nagasaki), different in origin, language, race and social condition, are united with each other and with the entire People of God in the saving mystery of Christ the Redeemer. Together with them, we too, gathered here with the Synod Fathers from almost every country of the world, sing to the Lamb the new song of the Book of Revelation:
>
> "Worthy are you to receive the scroll and to break open its seals, for you were slain and with your blood you purchased for God those from every tribe and tongue, people and nation. You made them a kingdom and priests for our God, and they will reign on earth" (Rev 5:9–10).
>
> The martyrs' message of supreme fidelity to Christ speaks to Europe, with its common Christian foundation laid by the Apostles Peter and Paul—Europe, which has been a seedbed of missionaries for two thousand years.
>
> It speaks to the Philippines, which was the place of immediate preparation and strengthening in faith for eleven of the new Saints—the Philippines which, as I remarked on the occasion of the martyrs' Beatification in Manila in 1981, from being evangelized is called to become an evangelizer in the great work of bringing the Gospel to the peoples of Asia. May this task of evangelization begin in Philippine families, following the example of Lorenzo Ruiz, husband and father of three children, who first collaborated with the Dominican Fathers in Manila and then shared their martyrdom in Nagasaki, and who is now *the first canonized Filipino saint.*[3]

---

[3] Ibid., October 26, 1987, pp. 9–10.

Blessed
Alain de Solminihac

Augustinian Canon
Regular, Abbot, Bishop

b. November 25, 1593, Belet
d. December 31, 1659, Mercuès

Beatified October 4, 1981

Though by human reckoning he had deserved to be canonized ages ago, Blessed Alain de Solminihac[1] was raised to the honors of the altar on October 4, 1981. During the "Century of Saints" in France he worked diligently as the abbot of Chancellade Abbey for thirteen years to bring about a great reform of the Canons Regular of Saint Augustine, and then for twenty-two years, from 1637 until his death on December 31, 1659, he was an exemplary Tridentine bishop of the Counter-Reformation in the manner of Saint Charles Borromeo.

This blessed was born on November 25, 1593, as the fourth child of an exemplary couple who belonged to the old landed nobility in France. The father, Jean de Solminihac, was Lord of Belet and Reyssidou and a loyal adherent to the Catholic faith; the mother, Marguerite de Marquessac, had, in addition to nobility of blood-line, a genuine nobility of soul and was deeply devout.

[1] K. Egger, *Der selige Alanus von Solminihac* (Rome, 1981); R. Darricau, "Alano de Solminihac, vescovo di Cahors", in *Bibliotheca sanctorum* 11:1295–1310.

As a young man Alain first aspired to the order of the Knights of Malta, in the hopes that a military career would not only allow him to serve as a knight, as was fitting for one of noble descent, but also would enable him to render to God the honor that was due to him. Very soon, however, he realized that he was in fact called to the clerical estate. This corresponded to the wishes of his uncle, Arnold de Solminihac, who was a Canon Regular of Saint Augustine and since 1583 had possessed a lucrative benefice as abbot of the Abbey of Our Lady of Chancellade near Périgueux and so was concerned that someone from his lineage should hold the same ecclesiastical office after him. This uncle had already invited three other nephews to accede to his wishes, but all three had declined. So he turned to his nephew Alain. Alain accepted his uncle's invitation, trusting that this was in keeping with the will of God. Through nepotism, then, Alain de Solminihac became a Canon Regular of Saint Augustine and, it was understood, the future abbot of Chancellade Abbey. In this instance the effects of nepotism were not negative but rather, much as in the case of Saint Charles Borromeo, very positive. For the prospective abbot of this abbey was not concerned about the lucrative benefice; rather, he wanted to govern the abbey someday as a truly exemplary abbot and to bring it from its lamentable state of ruin back to its former heights. Therefore Alain de Solminihac went first to Cahors to complete the necessary academic formation in civil law and canon law. Then he began in earnest the novitiate at the Abbey of Chancellade, which was meant to be his.

On July 28, 1616, he professed temporary vows; on September 17, 1616, he was ordained a subdeacon; on March 25, 1617, a deacon; and on September 22, 1618, a priest. With that he could now acquire the rank of abbot, at the head of a monastery, which he viewed, not as a source of income, but as a responsibility to which he would devote his efforts unselfishly, in order to bring it back from spiritual, intellectual, and material decline to new heights. To succeed in this—he sensed immediately—still other special qualities were required of an abbot: solid theological training, genuine spirituality of the kind that ought to be present in a community of canons regular, and in addition special leadership qualities. On this account the abbot-elect went next to Paris for the years 1618 to 1622 in order to complete what was still lacking in his priestly education and formation. During these years he heard outstanding professors at the Sorbonne and came into contact with men of importance in the spiritual life, for example, Saint Vincent de Paul; Father Olier, the founder of the Seminary of Saint Sulpice; and Charles Fauré, who was to become one of the reformers of the Canons Regular of Saint Augustine. Alain de Solminihac heard famous preachers in Paris, too, among them Saint Francis de Sales, who preached the Lenten mission in Paris in the year 1619 and with whom the future abbot of Chancellade was able to engage in valuable discussions. All this helped the young priest in governing and reforming his abbey. Immediately before taking office in 1619, Alain de Solminihac made the thirty-day Spiritual Exercises [of Saint Ignatius Loyola]. He then went to work in his abbey, which at that time lay in ruins in every respect and which housed in the monastery building itself only one canon; a few others lived in affiliated communities.

In 1623 Alain de Solminihac introduced new constitutions for his abbey, every word of which he himself had composed; in their essential points they contained all that was necessary for a genuine reform of this community of Canons Regular of Saint Augustine. Slowly but surely aspiring novices arrived, and the abbot personally and diligently made every effort to provide for their spiritual formation. At last, increasing progress was made in the abbey. The reform of the abbey succeeded and even began to radiate a positive influence beyond its own walls, so that acknowledged masters of the spiritual life like Saint Vincent de Paul praised the example it was setting for other religious communities.

As a result of the prominence that the abbey achieved, the abbot eventually acquired all sorts of duties and positions in the Church of France. Among his other responsibilities, he was the visitator of various monasteries, not only of his own order but also of other religious communities.

On two occasions already Abbot Alain had been sought as a candidate for an episcopal see: the first time in 1628, when the bishop of Bazas, Jean Jaubert de Barrault, wanted to resign from his office in favor of the abbot of Chancellade; then a second time in 1636 when the diocese of Lavaur was offered to the highly meritorious superior and reformer. He declined again and again out of modesty and because he did not want to abandon his reformed abbey.

In the same year of 1636, however, the abbot was nominated bishop of Cahors on the recommendation of Cardinal Richelieu. This time he could not refuse. Nevertheless, he managed to obtain permission to continue governing the abbey of Chancellade during his first years as bishop of Cahors.

In the spirit of Saint Charles Borromeo, whom Alain de Solminihac deliberately took as a model, he now devoted himself and all his efforts to the diocese entrusted to him after he was consecrated a bishop on September 27, 1637, in the church of Sainte-Geneviève in Paris by the archbishop of Toulouse. From his reformed abbey he brought with him eight especially zealous canons regular, and he assigned to them important duties as collaborators in governing the diocese of Cahors.

What Alain de Solminihac attempted to achieve in his diocese during the next twenty-two years resembles in many respects what Saint Charles Borromeo accomplished in the archdiocese of Milan. As early as April 21, 1638, Bishop Alain was presiding over a diocesan synod, which was followed by still others, resulting in important decrees of reform. Immediately after the first diocesan synod the bishop began a visitation of his large and extensive diocese, which comprised eight hundred parishes; he visited all of them systematically nine times in the course of twenty-two years. His work as chief shepherd, which was entirely free from self-interest and ambition, as well as from any taint of Gallicanism, was resolutely opposed to Jansenism and the weakening of clerical discipline and was directed toward strengthening the faith and morals of the people in the diocese. Through popular missions, clergy conferences, a new division of the diocese into deaneries, and the foundation of a seminary for the education of priests as called for by the Council of Trent—erected in 1642, it was one of the first in all of France—through the creation of hospitals and orphanages and through the prompt assistance and pastoral love that he showed for the people of his diocese, especially in times of need (civil wars, plague, and other catastrophes), he renewed his diocese.

In the midst of these duties he remained a contemplative, a man of prayer; in every respect he was an exemplary, humble bishop who was faithful and obedient to the successor of Peter (attributes that in those days in France could not be taken for granted) and who affirmed all the decrees and instructions of the Holy See and conscientiously carried them out. He used to say, "When the Pope has spoken, nothing more is needed except submission and obedience, without searching into reasons and motives or critically examining what has been commanded. Indeed, when we received Holy Orders we promised our obedience." [2]

At the beatification ceremony on October 4, 1981, in Saint Peter's Square in Rome, Pope John Paul II said:

> Alain de Solminihac, who came from an old family in Périgord, whose motto was "Faith and Valour", had first considered the Knights of Malta. But in 1613, at the age of twenty, he decides to enter Chancellade Abbey, near Périgueux, run by the Canons Regular of St. Augustine. After his ordination, he continues theology and spirituality studies in Paris. On the Epiphany, 1623, he receives the abbatial Blessing and courageously undertakes the material and spiritual restoration of his Abbey. It was the age of the implementation of the Council of Trent. This example had great repercussions in the region and far beyond it. . . .
>
> In 1636, the reputation of zeal and holiness that the Abbot of Chancellade had won, caused him to be appointed to the see of Cahors by Pope Urban VIII. A fervent admirer of the conciliar

---

[2] Chastenet, *La Vie de Mgr. Alain* (Cahors, 1663).

apostolate of the holy archbishop of Milan, Charles Borromeo, Bishop Solminihac also made the decision to give his diocese the image and the vitality so eagerly desired by the Council of Trent. His twenty-two years of episcopate in Quercy were a continual development of important and effective activities: the convocation of a diocesan synod, the setting up of a weekly episcopal council, systematic visitation of the eight hundred parishes of the diocese, each of which he saw nine times, the creation of a seminary entrusted to the Lazarists, the multiplication of parish missions, the development of eucharistic worship at a time when Jansenism was beginning to spread, the promotion or foundation of works of charity for the aged and for orphans, for the sick and victims of the plague. Three years before his death, he himself preached the 1656 Jubilee, both to convert his people and to make them aware of the particular mission of the Bishop of Rome, the guardian of communion between the Churches. In short, a word taken from Psalm 69 would sum up perfectly the pastoral life of this 17th-century bishop: "Zeal for thy house has consumed me." The remarkable figure of Alain de Solminihac certainly deserved to be highlighted by the Church, which he served so ardently. May the bishops of France and of all countries find in the life of Blessed Alain de Solminihac the courage to evangelize the modern world fearlessly! [3]

[3] "Message of Christian Joy: Love God and Your Neighbour", *L'Osservatore romano*, October 12, 1981, p. 1.

Blessed [Saint] Claudine Thévenet

Foundress

b. March 30, 1774, Lyons
d. February 3, 1837, Lyons

Beatified October 4, 1981
[Canonized March 21, 1993]

Claudine Thévenet,[1] the second daughter born to Philibert Thévenet and Marie Antoinette (née Guyot), first saw the light of day on March 30, 1774, in Lyons. Until 1789, the year the French Revolution broke out, Claudine Thévenet stayed in the abbey of Saint-Pierre-les-Nonnains for her education. Soon afterward she experienced a terrible shock.

On January 5, 1794, she appeared on the scene, by chance it seemed, during the "Massacre of Lyons" as her two brothers Louis Antoine and François were being led off to the place of execution and as the young men were cruelly put to death. As a consequence of the frightful, horrible things she witnessed, for the rest of her life she experienced a spasmodic shaking of the head and oppressive shortness of breath. Yet her two brothers had called to her before their execution: "Forgive, as we also forgive." This became her mainstay.

After she had magnanimously forgiven her brothers' murderers, Claudine Thévenet became very active in supporting the orphans

[1] G. M. C. Montesinos, *Da quella notte a Pierres-Plantées: Vita e opera di Claudina Thévenet* (Rome, 1974).

and the poor of her parish in Lyons, working alone and in isolation at first, but increasingly in cooperation with other young women of the same age. She soon became the soul of all the charitable activities in her parish. Her advisor in these matters was the enterprising Father André Coindre, who stood by her constantly, first of all in starting a Pious Union of the Most Sacred Heart of Jesus. The first seven members of this pious association felt more and more that they were being called to religious life. So Claudine Thévenet left her parents' house two years later to call into being the Congregation of Jesus and Mary.

Through the initiative of Claudine Thévenet, whose name now in religion was Sister Marie de Saint Ignace, a boarding school was founded in Fourvière for girls from well-to-do families, then an institution for orphans and abandoned girls, so as to provide for all of them, in the time of religious and moral crisis after the French Revolution, a solid education in the faith and character formation. This congregation of nuns with their boarding schools for girls developed quite well, until one day in 1835 the danger arose that the congregation of Blessed Claudine Thévenet would have to be united with the foundation of Saint Madeleine Sophie Barat, the Congregation of the Sacred Heart. This danger eventually passed, but it left Blessed Claudine badly shaken. She expended more and more of her strength on the extension and development of her congregation, until on February 3, 1837, her motherly, loving heart came to a halt.

At the beatification ceremony on October 4, 1981, Pope John Paul II said the following about this new blessed:

Claudine Thévenet lived in Lyons all her life. Her adolescence was upset by the French Revolution, which shook her native city so violently. One morning in January 1794, this 19-year-old girl recognized her two brothers, Louis and François, in a procession of people condemned to death. She had the courage to accompany them to the place of execution and to receive their last words: ". . . , forgive as we forgive!"

This event was certainly a decisive element in the vocation of Claudine, who already felt such sympathy for all the misery accumulated by the storm of the Revolution. She dreamed of becoming a messenger of God's mercy and forgiveness in a torn society, and of dedicating her life to the education of the young, especially the poorest, whose state of abandonment is more than we can imagine.

That is why, with the enlightened support of Father Coindre, Claudine founded a Pious Union in 1816, which would become two years later the Congregation of Jesus and Mary. Today, for the greater joy of the Church, the Daughters of Mother Thévenet amount to over two thousand, present in all continents and really living by her spirit. Schools and colleges, hostels for girls and for old persons, catechetical and family apostolates, dispensaries and houses of prayer have only one purpose: to make Jesus and Mary known, while working for the social advancement of the poor. . . .

Claudine Thévenet presents herself to us as a model of love and forgiveness. "Let charity be the apple of your eye," she still says now as she liked to repeat to her Sisters. "Be ready to suffer everything from others and never to cause anyone suffering." [2]

---

[2] "Message of Christian Joy: Love God and Your Neighbour", *L'Osservatore romano*, October 12, 1981, p. 12.

Blessed Luigi Scrosoppi

Oratorian

b. August 4, 1804, Udine
d. April 3, 1884, Udine

Beatified October 4, 1981

On October 4, 1981, Pope John Paul II beatified an excellent priest who was noted for his extraordinary charitable and educational work in Udine, the city of his birth: the Oratorian Luigi Scrosoppi,[1] who was born on August 4, 1804, in Udine as the son of the merchant Domingo Scrosoppi and of Antonia, the former Signora Filaferro, who had been widowed and remarried. After two of his stepbrothers joined the Oratory in Udine between 1809 and 1825, Blessed Luigi Scrosoppi, following their example, entered the Oratory in Udine in his turn and became a shining light of this priestly society. On March 27, 1827, he was ordained a priest. He immediately devoted himself to the development and extension of an orphanage that had been founded by two elderly, saintly priests in Borgo Ronchi and entrusted to the care of the Oratorian Carlo Filaferro. Through the energetic collaboration of Luigi Scrosoppi, the tiny orphanage eventually became an imposing institution with a school and a dormitory for ninety-five resident orphan girls and 230 externs.

[1] P. Colombara, *Un apostolo della carità, P. Luigi Scrosoppi* (Bergamo, 1929); C. Gasbarri, "Scrosoppi, Luigi", in *Bibliotheca sanctorum* 11:753–54.

Along the way there were many difficulties, of both the financial and also the pedagogical sort, which were nevertheless gradually overcome, a major step occurring in February 1837, when seven young women banded together to form a congregation, the Sisters of Providence, dedicated to the education of orphan girls.

When Father Carlo Filaferro died in 1854, Father Luigi Scrosoppi became his successor as superior of the Oratory in Udine and remained in the position until 1866, when the priestly society was suppressed and dissolved. During this time, though, Blessed Luigi Scrosoppi was able to expand the congregation of nuns and to obtain for it ecclesiastical recognition and canonical approval by Pope Pius IX on August 7, 1862.

The efforts of this selfless priest reached far beyond the institutes he founded or directed and gave an authentic example of Christian charity. He also founded in Udine an institute for deaf-mutes and supported with his own income the publication of the newspaper *Giornale del Popolo* [People's daily], which had a Christian orientation; he was of great help to the Poor Clares in Udine, took care of impoverished priests, especially former missionaries who had become poor and sick, and staunchly supported needy candidates for the priesthood. There was not a single charitable work in Udine that the noble Oratorian Luigi Scrosoppi did not support as an open-hearted, open-handed priest.

After a long, painful illness, which he endured with exemplary resignation to the will of God, Luigi Scrosoppi died on April 3, 1884.

At his beatification Pope John Paul II said the following:

Luigi Scrosoppi, of Udine, ordained a priest in 1827, dedicated himself to a tireless apostolate, animated and driven by the charity of Christ. He set up the "House for Foundling Girls" or "Institute of Providence" for the human and Christian formation of girls; he opened the "Home" for former pupils who were unemployed; he began the Work for Deaf-mute Girls, and founded the Sisters of Providence under the protection of Saint

Cajetan. Father Luigi entered the Congregation of the Oratory and made it a dynamic centre from which spiritual life radiated.

In his life, spent entirely for souls, he had three great loves: Jesus, the Church and the Pope, [and] the "little ones".

From a very early age he chose Christ as his teacher and loved him, contemplating him poor and humble at Bethlehem; a worker at Nazareth; suffering and a victim at Gethsemane and on Golgotha; present in the Eucharist. "I want to be faithful to him", he wrote, "perfectly attached to him on the way to heaven and to be a copy of him."

His love for the Church was manifested in complete fidelity to Church laws; in his apostolate, which knew no pauses or hesitations; in docile acceptance of the Magisterium.

Father Scrosoppi spent literally all his life in the practice of charity towards his neighbour, especially towards the smallest and most abandoned. He distributed the wealth of his family for the poor. "The poor and the sick are our masters and represent the very person of Jesus Christ": these are his words; but they are also, and more, his life.

At the basis of his multiple pastoral and charitable activity, there is a deep spirituality; his day was one continual prayer: meditation, visits to the Blessed Sacrament, recitation of the Breviary, daily "Via Crucis", Rosary and, finally, long prayer at night. In this way he set the faithful, priests and religious a luminous and effective example of a well-balanced synthesis between contemplative life and active life.[2]

---

[2] "Message of Christian Joy: Love God and Your Neighbour", *L'Osservatore romano*, October 12, 1981, pp. 1, 12.

Blessed Maria Repetto

Religious, Portress

b. November 1, 1807, Voltaggio
d. January 5, 1890, Genoa

Beatified October 4, 1981

Blessed Maria Repetto,[1] who was raised to the honors of the altar on October 4, 1981, was the first born of the eight children of the notary Giovanni Battista Repetto and Teresa (née Gazzale). After her birth on November 1, 1807, in Voltaggio (Alessandria, arch-diocese of Genoa), she grew up in a family in which faith and piety were very highly valued. One proof of this is the fact that, of the seven daughters, four chose religious life, and the only son became a zealous priest.

At twenty-one years of age Maria Repetto left her parents' house and entered the cloister of Our Lady of Refuge on Monte Calvario in Genoa. She belonged now to a community of Sisters that offered women the opportunity to consecrate themselves to God by private vows and to live a secluded life of service, caring for the elderly, the orphaned, and the sick. In a note appended to her request for admission, Maria Repetto had requested the governing council that she never be obliged to perform any duties outside of

---

[1] L. Traverso, *Un fiore di Monte Calvario, Suor Maria Repetto, la Monaca Santa* (Genoa, 1949).

the community. She wanted to lead a life that was completely and utterly hidden. For many years, in fact, she was employed in mending and embroidering at the workshop within the cloister and finally as portress.

Her path to perfection and holiness, which she followed with self-sacrificing courage, was characterized by the utmost simplicity and childlike devotion as well as by absolute faithfulness in completing the modest tasks that were assigned to her.

Although she lived in complete seclusion, the virtuous life of this consecrated woman of God had an increasing influence that radiated even beyond her community. The result was that poor and needy people came more and more often to the cloister. Here the portress Maria Repetto could pursue her charitable apostolate, which to a certain extent complemented the apostolate conducted in those years by the Capuchin friar Saint Francesco Maria de Camporosso in the streets of Genoa. Whereas this Capuchin was called *Padre santo* (the saintly father) by the inhabitants of the city, Maria Repetto was honored with the title *Monaca santa* (the saintly nun).

Especially characteristic features of the spirituality of this blessed include a boundless confidence in the intercession of Saint Joseph, to whom she preferred to direct her prayers for the intentions communicated to her by the sick, the needy, and those seeking advice. She also liked to give out little holy cards of Saint Joseph (*Giuseppini*) to the people who asked for help. Furthermore, the spirituality of Blessed Maria Repetto was stamped by her concern for providing poor churches with the requisite liturgical furnishings, because she prized highly the beauty of the churches and of the liturgies that were celebrated in them.

Only twice during her life did the blessed leave her cloister, namely, during the cholera epidemics of 1835 and 1854. In fact, on those occasions she asked to be employed caring for the sick. She herself then spent the last years of her life in the infirmary of the cloister, until she fell asleep in the Lord on January 5, 1890.

A short summary of the life of Blessed Maria Maddalena Pellegrina Repetto was given by Pope John Paul II during the beatification ceremony on October 4, 1981, in the following words:

> Maria Repetto, at the age of 21, enters the Congregation of the Sisters of Our Lady of Refuge, at Monte Calvario, in Genoa. In the many serious cholera epidemics which broke out in the city, she rushes, fearless, to the bedside of the sick. The fame of the "holy nun" grows every day and, when she assumes the office of portress, she continues to bestow the treasures of her deep spirituality on all those who flock to her for help and advice.
>
> Right from her youth, Maria Repetto learned and lived a great truth, which she has transmitted also to us: Jesus must be contemplated, loved and served in the poor, at all moments of our life. She gives everything she has: her savings, her possessions, her words, her time, her smile. "To serve Christ's poor" was the programme of her Institute; a programme which she carried out in 50 years of religious life, serving Jesus above all, growing in the perfection of love, reminding herself to "be first and foremost a religious!" and serving the poor, because Christ lives in the poor.[2]

---

[2] "Message of Christian Joy: Love God and Your Neighbour", *L'Osservatore romano*, October 12, 1981, p. 12.

Blessed [Saint] Riccardo Pampuri

Hospitaller

b. August 2, 1897, Trivolzio
d. May 1, 1930, Milan

Beatified October 4, 1981
[Canonized November 2, 1989]

In our time, too, the Hospitaller order of Saint John of God, with its strenuous work of caring for the sick, is a field in which genuine sanctity can grow and mature; Pope John Paul II has confirmed this by beatifying two members of the order, namely, Riccardo Erminio Filippo Pampuri,[1] on October 4, 1981, and Benedetto Angelo Menni, on June 23, 1985.

The first-named, who has meanwhile been canonized as well, on November 1, 1989, was born on August 2, 1897, as the tenth of eleven children of the parents Innocente and Angela Campari in Trivolzio near Pavia; the following day he was baptized with the name Erminio Filippo. The child lost his mother at the age of three and was entrusted to his grandfather and to the sisters of his mother in Torinno near Trivolzio, who raised him. At the age of eleven the boy lost his father also in a traffic accident.

---

[1] P. Chiminelli, *Fra Riccardo Pampuri, Giovane d'Azione Cattolica, Medico, Religioso dei Fatebenefratelli* (Rome, 1974); Generalpostulation des Ordens der Barmherzigen Brüder: *Sein Beispiel leuchtet: Geschichte eines Arztes, der hl. Richard Pampuri* (Munich, 1989).

He attended secondary schools in Pavia and after his final examinations began the study of medicine in the same city. In 1921 he graduated with distinction as a doctor of medicine. Soon afterward he became a general practitioner in Morimondo near Milan and, as such, was a good Samaritan for the people there and, furthermore, a zealous lay apostle, who founded in his parish a Catholic Action youth group and a Saint Pius X Association. At any time of the day or night he was on call for the sick people in that locality, and to the poor he not only made available his skills as a physician but also gave them, free of charge, medicine and food, blankets, clothing, and money, but above all spiritual comfort and encouragement in their faith through his word and example.

In 1927 Dr. Erminio Filippo Pampuri entered the order of the Hospitaller Brothers of Saint John of God in Brescia and took the religious name Riccardo. After making his religious vows, Brother Riccardo soon became director of the Institute for Dentistry at Saint Ursula Hospital in Brescia. After only a short time "the little doctor" (*dottorino*) met with so much honor and respect on the part of his patients that, for example, mothers came to him with their children and asked him to lay his healing hands upon the little ones and to bless them.

At age thirty-three Brother Riccardo fell ill with a very unusual inflammation of the lungs, the result of a pleurisy he had contracted while completing his military service. In Saint Joseph Hospital in Milan, which was run by his order, he died on May 1, 1930, in the odor of sanctity, and his reputation was very soon corroborated by remarkable favors and miraculous cures obtained through his intercession. Pope John Paul II beatified this saintly doctor, who died at the age of thirty-three—the same age as our Lord Jesus Christ—on October 4, 1981. On that occasion the Pope said:

Erminio Filippo Pampuri, the tenth of eleven children, is a general practitioner at the age of 24. At the age of 30 he enters the Hospitaller Order of St. John of God (*Fatebenefratelli*). Only three years later, he dies.

He is an extraordinary figure, near us in time, but even closer to our problems and our sensitivity. We admire in Erminio Filippo, who became Fra Riccardo Pampuri in the order, the young Christian layman, committed to bearing witness in student circles, as an active member of the "Severino Boezio" University Club and a member of the Conference of St. Vincent de Paul; the dynamic doctor, animated by intense and concrete charity for the sick and the poor, in whom he saw the face of the suffering Christ. He carried out literally the words that he wrote to his sister, a nun, when he was a general practitioner: "Pray that pride, selfishness and any other evil passion will not prevent me from always seeing the suffering Christ in my patients, treating him and comforting him. With this thought always alive in my mind, how sweet and how fruitful the practice of my profession should appear to me!"

We admire him also as an upright Religious of a well-deserving Order, who, in the spirit of its Founder, St. John of God, made charity to God and brothers his own specific mission and his own original charism. "I want to serve you, God, for the future, with perseverance and supreme love: in my Superiors, in confreres, in your beloved sick: give me the grace to serve them as I would serve you": thus he wrote in his resolutions in preparation for religious profession.

The short but intense life of Fra Riccardo Pampuri is an incentive for the whole People of God, but especially for the young, for doctors and for religious.

He calls the young people of today to live Christian faith joyfully and courageously: continually listening to the Word of God, in generous consistency with the requirements of Christ's message, in donation to brothers.

He calls doctors, his colleagues, to carry out their delicate art with commitment, animating it with Christian, human and professional ideals, so that it may be a real mission of social service, fraternal charity and real human promotion.

Fra Riccardo urges men and women religious, especially those who, in humility and concealment, carry out their consecrated life amid the wards of hospitals and clinics, to live the original spirit of their Institute, in love of God and needy brothers.[2]

---

[2] "Message of Christian Joy: Love God and Your Neighbour", *L'Osservatore romano*, October 12, 1981, p. 12.

The physician and Hospitaller Brother Riccardo Pampuri, who died at the age of almost thirty-three years, was canonized by Pope John Paul II on the feast of All Saints 1989 on the basis of another miracle that God worked through the intercession of the blessed. On this occasion the Pope said the following about the new saint:

"Blessed are the merciful: . . . blessed are the pure of heart" (Mt 5:7–8). In just thirty-three years, like Christ, whom he loved above all else, St. Riccardo Pampuri's life was totally a gift to God and to his brothers and sisters, as a young apostle among the university students, among the soldiers in the trenches during the horrors of the [First World] War, among the faithful of the parish where he served as the district doctor. Following then his personal vocation, he entered the Order of the Brothers of St. John of God, because he was attracted by the specific ministry of this lay religious family. This community was established to offer a service of charity, one that was indeed heroic, to the poorest among the sick and the suffering.

In a community that made mercy the principal motto of its own ministry, St. Riccardo felt that he had to respond with a new sign and a new availability to Christ "with a correspondence that was always more ready and generous, with an abandonment that was always more total, always more perfect, towards the most Sacred Heart of Jesus" (Letter to his sister, October 1923).

It is necessary, however, to recall that St. Riccardo began his journey towards sanctification in the context of an intense lay spirituality, as proposed by Catholic Action. For this reason, both in his adolescence as well as in his student and professional life, he committed himself to the work of formation with the help of careful spiritual direction, making the Spiritual Exercises a strong point of reference for himself and drawing from his Eucharistic piety the energy necessary to go on despite the difficulties. Above all, he penetrated the message of Gospel charity in the light of meditation and prayer, spending intense periods of contemplation before the Eucharist and then dedicating himself with a particularly acute sensitivity to those suffering in any way.

How could anyone not be moved by the words that St. Riccardo said to his spiritual director in one of their last meetings: "Father, how will God receive me? . . . I have loved him much and I love him so much." In this intense love is found the supreme value of the charism of a genuine Brother of the Order of St. John of God, whose vocation consists precisely in proposing anew the image of Christ to all whom he meets along the way, in a relationship composed of a selfless love and nourished at the font of a pure heart.

"*Who has the right to climb the mountain of the Lord*, who the right to stand in his holy place?" (Ps 24:3); the Church asks this question with the words of the Psalmist in today's solemnity. And the response is: "He whose hands are clean, whose heart is pure. . . ." Such a man was . . . St. Riccardo Pampuri.[3]

---

[3] "Homily at Canonization", *L'Osservatore romano*, November 20, 1989, pp. 6, 8.

Blessed
Maria Angela Astorch

Religious, Foundress

b. September 1, 1592, Barcelona
d. December 2, 1665, Murcia

Beatified May 23, 1982

Ten years after the death of Saint Teresa of Avila (October 4, 1582), Barcelona, Spain, became the birthplace of Angela Astorch,[1] who likewise as a religious led a life of sanctity, in her case not among the Carmelites but, rather, in the order of the Poor Clare Capuchins. Like Saint Teresa she founded several new houses of her religious community. Moreover, she was likewise notable for her strong ecclesiastical sense, so that one could place on her lips also the words "After all, I am a daughter of the Church."

Maria Angela Astorch, who was born on September 1, 1592, lost her parents at the age of five. The little girl then came down with a very serious illness and actually died of it. According to contemporary reports—her first biographers, including the famous Jesuit Father Luis Ignacio Zevallos, have attested to their reliability and truthfulness—the girl was brought back to life again by the Servant of God Mother Angela Margarita Serafina, who a few years previously had started the first convent of Capuchin Sisters in Barcelona.

[1] V. de Peralta, "La Venerabile Sor Angela Maria Astorch", *Estudios Franciscanos* 22 (1919): 426–45; P. Lechner, *Leben der Heiligen aus dem Orden der Kapuziner*, vol. 3 (Munich, 1864), 299–329.

This same Capuchin convent took Angela in when she was eleven years old. As she matured, she arrived at the decision to consecrate herself completely to God as a religious according to the rule of Saint Clare of Assisi. On September 8, 1609, she was permitted to take the three vows of the order.

The young nun soon distinguished herself by the various virtues demanded of the Sisters of her order and by her great fidelity to the ideal of the seraphic Saint of Assisi. Already at the age of twenty-five she was commissioned to found a Capuchin convent in Saragossa, where she then assumed the office of novice mistress and finally that of abbess. Then she founded another convent in Murcia. Through the good example and enterprising spirit of Abbess Angela, this convent soon achieved a remarkable splendor. She composed mystical writings, which, though unpublished, are still stored in the archives of the convent in Murcia; in these works the abbess provided her Sisters with a valuable manual on attaining Christian perfection.

After a life of prayer and penance, characterized above all by the faithful recitation of the liturgical prayers of the Divine Office, Abbess Angela died—highly respected and admired on account of her heroic virtues and her mystical experiences—on December 2, 1665, during the seventy-third year of her life and the twentieth year of her successful service as abbess in Murcia.

Pope John Paul II spoke of this Spanish Sister at the beatification ceremony on May 23, 1982, in Saint Peter's Square in Rome:

Maria Angela Astorch [is] another example of sanctity that has matured in Spain. She belongs to the family of religious known as the Poor Clare Capuchins.

In the successive stages of her life, first as a simple religious, then as a young mistress of novices, later in charge of the formation of the professed, and finally as abbess, she left everywhere, in Barcelona, Zaragoza, Seville and Murcia, a wonderful witness of fidelity to her own consecration and love for the Church.

Gifted with an intelligence above the ordinary, she found support in the solidity of the revealed word and of ecclesiastical writers which she studied and knew in depth. This gave her in turn a sound understanding both in theory and practise of the ways of that spirituality which lives in intimate union with the Church, especially by means of the liturgy, the sacred texts and the divine office. For this reason we might describe her as a mystic of the breviary.

In the work of formation she used that noble way which God had made use of in her case. For this reason she was able to respect the individuality of each person, helping the one concerned "to keep in step with God", which means something different for each one. In this way her profound understanding did not become inert tolerance.

Maria Angela is, for this reason, a figure to whom we should look with attention in our times. From her we can learn to respect the ways of man and at the same time make men open to the ways of God.[2]

---

[2] "Signs of God's Presence among Men", *L'Osservatore romano*, June 14, 1982, p. 6.

Blessed Marie Rivier

Foundress, Congregation
of the Sisters of the
Presentation of Mary

*b. December 19, 1768, Montpezat-
sous-Bauzon*

*d. February 3, 1838, Bourg-Saint-
Andéol*

Beatified May 23, 1982

It was a miracle that holiness should blossom at the time of the French Revolution, yet such a flower of sanctity was beatified on May 23, 1982: the foundress of the Congregation of Sisters of the Presentation of Mary, Marie Rivier.[1]

She was born on December 19, 1768, in Montpezat-sous-Bauzon (département Ardèche, France). Toward the end of April 1770, at the age of sixteen months, she fell out of bed and injured her hip and ankle so badly that she completely lost the use of her feet; she could not even stand, much less walk. Lying on her back, she would laboriously use her little hands to creep forward bit by bit. Her disability increased from day to day, because her legs developed slowly and became crooked. The child kept getting weaker and more frail. From her earliest childhood Marie had a tender love for the Blessed Mother, and when she had reached the age of six the thought occurred to her to entrust herself unreservedly to the Blessed Virgin for life. The Mother of God answered Marie's

[1] A. Moulard, *La Vie apostolique de la vénérable Marie Rivier, fondatrice des Soeurs de la Présentation, 1768–1838* (Paris, 1934).

confident act of devotion on August 15, 1777, by obtaining for her a complete and miraculous healing at the age of nine.

Now it was up to the girl who had been miraculously restored to health to find the right way of expressing her thanks to Mary. First Marie thought of a life of continual prayer in a wilderness retreat. This intention, though, quickly turned out to be impractical. Since she could not become a hermit, she became a "woman apostle", as she was characterized by Pope Pius IX. She recalled the resolution she had made as a little child to lead many children to their heavenly Mother. Now she put this into practice. She looked up other girls her own age, gathered them around, and began to instruct them in the truths of the faith. Soon her comrades were calling her the *petite Maman*, and they respected and loved her accordingly. Above all, Marie took care of poor, needy, and sick children.

The reception of her First Holy Communion awakened in this darling of Mary an ever-stronger yearning to belong completely to God. Therefore she was very happy when she arrived, together with an older sister, at the boarding school of the Sisters of Notre Dame in Pradelles (Upper Loire region). After finishing her studies with these nuns, she asked to be admitted to their congregation. When she did not receive permission, however, she promptly resolved: "If these Sisters don't want me in their religious community, I'll start one myself."

The time was not yet ripe, and so at first the young teacher founded a school, where from the very beginning she gave numerous children the best possible instruction and training. Many parents personally brought their children to this school so they could observe the pedagogical talents of the young teacher. As Marie Rivier saw it, the proof of her pedagogical talents was not only her pupils' success in learning but also their piety and goodness. Later she admitted, "Of all that I have done and accomplished in my life, what gives me the most comfort is the fact that in my youth I devoted myself to the education of children, so as to instruct them well and to lead them to God. Some of my pupils went on to be especially zealous Christians."

Then in 1789 the French Revolution broke out and seemingly destroyed the entire work of the now twenty-one-year-old schoolteacher. In concealment, however, the work continued to grow and finally developed into the Congregation of Sisters of the Presentation of Mary; at the death of this Frenchwoman, whose bravery and organizational talent have been compared with those of Napoleon, her community had already spread to 130 houses in twelve départements in France.

After the outbreak of the Revolution, Marie Rivier had to leave her native village of Montpezat and flee to the neighboring village of Thueyts. Here she became acquainted with the Sulpician priest Father M. Pontanier, who likewise had fled from the revolutionary dictators and who from then on was her strong support in the development and extension of her work.

In Thueyts she began again to instruct many children and also devoted herself more and more to religious education for adults, along the lines of evangelization. Sunday after Sunday great crowds of people gathered around her, from neighboring villages too, to hear this brave schoolteacher explain the truths of the catechism. She was joined by like-minded assistants. On the feast of the Presentation of the Blessed Virgin Mary in 1796, while Father Pontanier celebrated Holy Mass secretly in an attic of the school building, Marie Rivier promised, in the presence of her assistants and pupils, "to consecrate herself and her work completely to the Queen of Heaven". That was the start of the congregation of Sisters that she had planned. One year later, on November 21, 1797, the first "Presentines", together with their foundress, promised to live by the rule of the community, which Father Pontanier had drawn up provisionally. He immediately informed the archbishop of Vienne, François-Charles d'Aviau (who during the French Revolution was also apostolic administrator of the diocese of Viviers), about the event. Soon afterward, on August 7, 1801, the saintly chief shepherd approved the rule and the newly formed community, which from then on developed magnificently. The house in Thueyts soon was too small. In 1815 the former convent of the Visitation Sisters in Bourg-Saint-Andéol (Ardèche) was obtained. From there Marie Rivier guided and directed the work, which grew mightily. She remained the soul of this teaching apostolate and was highly respected as Mother, Foundress, and General Superior of the Congregation of Sisters of the Presentation until she went home on February 3, 1838.

Pope John Paul II, at the beatification of Mother Marie Rivier on May 23, 1982, praised this courageous woman in the following words:

Let us now look at Blessed Marie Rivier whom Pius IX called the "woman-apostle". It was in fact the ardour of her apostolate that struck her contemporaries, during and after the French Revolution. On fire from her childhood with the idea of teaching the young, to teach them, as a "little mother", to love God, she later founded the Sisters of the Presentation, especially to teach the young to live in the faith, with a particular interest in the poor and orphans, those who are abandoned or ignorant of God. She not only brought the young girls together but also wished to train good mothers, convinced of the evangelizing role of the family and the importance of religious initiation from an early age: "The whole of life lies in one's first impressions," she used to say. She was regarded as "the harvester of countless souls". And she used every means to that end: numerous village schools, missions, retreats which she preached herself, Sunday meetings. . . .

One is struck by her boldness, her tenacity, her expansive joy, her courage, "which was enough to fill a thousand lives". There were, however, many difficulties to discourage her: her childhood illness which lasted until she was healed on a feast of Our Lady, a lack of physical growth, a poor state of health throughout the seventy years of her life, the ignorance of religion that surrounded her. But her life demonstrates well the power of faith in a simple upright soul, which surrenders itself entirely to the grace of its baptism. She relied on God, who purified her through the cross. She prayed intensely to Mary and, with her, presented herself before God in a state of adoration and offering. Her spirituality is solidly theological and clearly apostolic: "Our vocation is Jesus Christ; we must fill ourselves with his spirit, so that his Kingdom may come, especially in the souls of children." [2]

---

[2] "Signs of God's Presence among Men", *L'Osservatore romano*, June 14, 1982, p. 7.

Blessed
Peter Donders

Missionary

b. October 27, 1805, Tilburg
d. January 14, 1887, Batavia

Beatified May 23, 1982

The marvelous accomplishments of the Catholic Church in the Netherlands for the foreign missions are embodied, so to speak, by the modest but truly heroic figure of the missionary Peter Donders, whom Pope John Paul II beatified on May 23, 1982. This was the crowning, as it were, of forty-five years of missionary work under the tropical sun of Dutch Guiana (Suriname), thirty of them among the lepers, that this priest from Holland spent in a truly valiant life of apostolic work, prayer, and penance in that far distant mission territory.

Peter Donders[1] first saw the light of day on October 27, 1805, in Tilburg in the Netherlands as the son of the weaver Arnold Donders and of Petronilla (née Van den Brekel). He learned his father's trade and practiced it, too, until he discovered his vocation to the priesthood and finally studied theology while continuing to work. On June 5, 1841, at the age of thirty-five, he was ordained a priest in Oogstgeest.

---

[1] H. Helmer, *En groot Nederlander in Suriname. Lewen en werken van den Dienaar Gods Petrus Donders* (Tillburg, 1946).

Profoundly impressed by the words of the Letter to the Hebrews (5:1ff.), he left his homeland in 1842 to labor from then on in Suriname, under the tropical sun, for forty-five years as a missionary and to win immortal souls for Christ and for eternal salvation. In his pastoral work he devoted himself mainly to the poorest and most abandoned people, first to the lepers, then to the Indian immigrants and the so-called bush-Negroes, black people who came from Africa to Suriname and were supposed to toil on the plantations of the rich settlers as slave laborers but who ran away and led a wretched life in the rain forest.

In 1865, when the local apostolic vicariate was entrusted to the missionaries from the Redemptorist order, Peter Donders asked to be admitted to this order, and he was accepted. On June 27, 1867, he professed perpetual vows as a Redemptorist. As such he continued to work for the lepers, as he had done since 1856, and furthermore cared for the Indians and the bush-Negroes who had settled in his mission territory. Among the Indians Peter Donders had the greatest success with the tribe of the Arrovachs. On September 17, 1873, he wrote to his superior:

During the month of September I called on my dear Arrovachs. For six days I was together with them. They put all of their other business aside, so as not to miss any of my instructions. By God's goodness I was able to complete today the thirty-first year of my apostolic activity in this region. And I had the great joy of administering First Holy Communion to twenty persons, together with twenty-two others who had already made their First Holy Communion during the past year. If you had been there, surely you too would have marveled at the great devotion that these native people have displayed.

Besides the lepers, the Indians, and the bush-Negroes, Father Peter Donders of course extended his ministry to the white settlers as well; yet first and foremost his priestly love belonged to the lepers. Therefore it is right that the honorific title "Apostle of the

Lepers" has been ascribed to him in particular. From 1842 until 1856 he worked in the capital city, Paramaribo, and from 1883 to 1885 in Coronie, on the seacoast. A few ungrateful lepers succeeded in driving Father Donders for a while from Batavia. The reception that people gave him, however, when he returned on November 17, 1885, was much more festive.

As for the personal conduct of this extraordinarily zealous missionary, it simply must be mentioned that he led a life full of prayer and penance. By far the greater part of his workday was devoted, whenever possible, to prayer. As a rule he would also interrupt his rest at night so as to spend an entire hour in adoration kneeling before the tabernacle.

Pope John Paul II said the following in Dutch about this great missionary from the Netherlands at the beatification ceremony in Saint Peter's Square in Rome:

Peter Donders, born at the beginning of the last century in the Netherlands, spent a great part of his life in Suriname, where he proclaimed the Gospel to the slaves, Negroes and Indians.

He was known above all for his spiritual and bodily care of lepers, so much so that he is rightly called the apostle of the lepers.

We can say that he was an apostle of the poor. In fact, he was born into a poor family and had to lead the life of a worker before he could pursue his priestly vocation. He dedicated his whole priestly life to the poor.

In addition, he is an invitation and an incentive for the renewal and reflourishing of the missionary thrust which in the last century and in this one has made an exceptional contribution to the carrying out of the Church's missionary duty. Joining the Congregation of the Most Holy Redeemer late in life, he practised in an excellent way what St. Alphonsus proposed as an ideal for his religious: imitate the virtues and examples of the Redeemer in preaching the divine word to the poor.

He showed, through his life, how the proclamation of the

Good News of redemption, the liberation from sin, must find support and confirmation in an authentic evangelical life, a life of concrete love for one's neighbour, above all toward the most lowly of brothers and sisters in Christ.[2]

[2] "Signs of God's Presence among Men", *L'Osservatore romano*, June 14, 1982, p. 6.

Blessed Marie-Rose Durocher

Foundress of the Congregation of the Sisters of the Holy Names of Jesus and Mary

b. October 6, 1811, Saint-Antoine-sur-Richelieu
d. October 6, 1849, Longueuil

Beatified May 23, 1982

Among the blessed souls whom Pope John Paul II has beatified during the first ten years of his pontificate for the Church in Canada is also the foundress of the Congregation of Sisters of the Holy Names of Jesus and Mary, Marie-Rose Durocher.[1]

In the village of Saint-Antoine-sur-Richelieu in the Province of Quebec in Canada, she was born into a family of believers as the last of ten children. Three of her brothers became priests, and one of her sisters became a nun, as she did. Only a short life was granted to Eulalie-Mélanie (the name she received at baptism), for she died on her thirty-eighth birthday; still, what she accomplished for the Church in Canada is significant.

Because of her poor health, her desire to consecrate herself to God in religious life was frustrated three times. When her brother Théophile, who was a priest, was appointed pastor of Saint-Benoît, she moved in with him and served as his housekeeper; she did this again in his second parish in Beloeil. During this time—the years

[1] J. H. Pretot, *Vie de Mère Marie-Rose* (Montreal, 1895); A. Pesant, "Durocher, Eulalie-Mélanie", in *Dizionario degli Istituti di Perfezione*, vol. 3, col. 1000–1002.

1830 through 1842—Marie-Rose Durocher was not only a housekeeper but also a pastoral assistant in her brother's parish and beyond in the neighboring parishes. She organized charitable works and cooperated everywhere in the care of souls.

In 1841 Marie-Rose Durocher began to gather around her a group of girls whom she directed and formed into a Marian congregation—the first to be canonically established in Canada.

At that time there were still no schools in the rural areas of Canada; they existed only in the great cities of Quebec and Montreal. This lack of schools distressed the far-sighted pastoral assistant. She turned to Bishop Ignace Bourget, who had also taken to heart the cause of constructing rural schools. Encouraged by him and well advised by her spiritual director, Father Adrian Telmon, O.M.I., she developed a plan to recruit nuns from Marseille to start schools in Canada. There were, however, no nuns capable of starting and developing a Canadian school system who were ready to emigrate to Canada. So Marie-Rose Durocher set to work herself, with the bishop's help, founding a suitable religious community. By October 28, 1843, a congregation of Sisters of the Holy Names of Jesus and Mary was formed in Longueil; already on December 8, 1844, this religious community received canonical approval. It was the first congregation of school Sisters to be founded in Canada and the first to have a Canadian foundress. Marie-Rose Durocher headed her community for only a few years, unfortunately. Still, by her example and by her own solid spirituality, which was based on strong eucharistic and Marian devotion, this young, sickly woman was able to provide a firm foundation for the congregation she had founded. Thus even great difficulties, in particular those caused by the apostate Charles Chiniquy, could be overcome happily.

Pope John Paul II said the following about her at the beatification ceremony that took place on May 23, 1982:

Beyond the Atlantic, in Canada, we find another very apostolic figure in Blessed Marie-Rose Durocher. She was born into a large family, rich with consecrated souls. In search of her true vocation in the Church and unable, through her poor health, to enter the only two female communities that then existed in Quebec, she served for thirteen years in her brother's presbytery—one would say nowadays as a priest's housekeeper—not only concerned with keeping house, but also with receiving sick priests and seminarists, directing the charitable works of the parish and encouraging devotion to Mary among young girls. Then, at the request of the Bishop of Montreal, and with the encouragement of the Oblate Fathers of Mary Immaculate and following the example of the Brothers of the Christian Schools, she founded a new community to meet the need for teaching and religious education of young girls, especially in the poor country areas around Montreal: the Sisters of the Holy Names of Jesus and Mary. During the last six years of her short life, she gave a sufficiently good start to her work, so that it now flourishes in six countries.

So what was the spirit that presided over such an apostolate, so closely linked to the needs of the Church at the time of the "Catholic renaissance" in Canada, at the beginning of the last century? Especially complete readiness to fulfil the commitments demanded of her by her faith in Jesus, her love of the Church, and concern for the least cared for. It was the ecclesiastical superiors who noticed her abilities and entrusted her with her mission: authentic apostolate, today as yesterday, is not merely a question of personal charism, but of the call of the Church and incorporation in its pastoral apostolate. Marie-Rose Durocher acted with simplicity, prudence, humility and serenity. She refused to be halted by her personal problems of health or the initial difficulties in her new-born work. Her secret lay in prayer and self-forgetfulness, which, according to her bishop, reached the point of real sanctity.[2]

---

[2] "Signs of God's Presence among Men", *L'Osservatore romano*, June 14, 1982, p. 7.

Blessed André Bessette

Lay Brother, Porter

b. April 9, 1845, Saint-Grégoire-d'Iberville

d. January 6, 1937, Montreal

Beatified May 23, 1982

This Canadian apostle of devotion to Saint Joseph, with whose help he worked astonishing miracles, was born on April 9, 1845, in Saint-Grégoire-d'Iberville in the diocese of Montreal as the eighth of twelve children of a carpenter named Bessette. The newborn child was so weak that they feared for his life, and because of the emergency a layperson administered baptism. Yet Alfred Bessette, though always sickly, lived to be ninety-two years old and accomplished marvels during his long life.

In 1854, when Alfred Bessette[1] was nine years old, he lost his father, then his mother in 1857, when he was twelve. The orphan was taken in by his mother's sister, Marie-Rosalie Nadeau (née Foisy). She deepened and strengthened the religious foundation that the boy's devout mother had laid. Besides, a saintly pastor by the name of André Provençal took an interest in him. The priest instilled in him a fervent love for our eucharistic Savior and a great

---

[1] F. J. L. Sattel, F.M.S., *St. Josef, der Helfer und Tröster, und sein Diener Bruder Andreas* (Gröbenzell, 1977); E. Catta, *Le Frère André et l'Oratoire de Saint Joseph du Mont-Royal* (Montreal-Paris, 1965).

devotion to Saint Joseph. Again and again he urged him to call on the foster father of Jesus in every difficulty: "He will hear you and bless you. Someday you will thank him for many favors, for Saint Joseph is very powerful with God." So no one was surprised to see the boy praying often in front of the handsome statue of Saint Joseph in the parish church. He promised the saint that he would become more and more like him.

From 1858 to 1860 Alfred Bessette tried out various sorts of employment, for instance, as a shoemaker, a baker's apprentice, and even as a farm worker. All of these jobs, though, were too hard for a youth in such poor health. Then Father Provençal advised him, because of his piety, to try religious life and to apply to the Congregation of the Holy Cross in Montreal. He was admitted, because Father Provençal had recommended him as a future saint in whom God had already worked many miracles of grace. On December 27, 1870, Alfred Bessette received the religious habit, and, in gratitude to his pastor, André Provençal, he took the name André.

Brother André humbly undertook the lowliest tasks, practiced heroic patience and mortification, and wanted to be considered worthless by his confreres. "Those were his goals in life. He accomplished them with astonishing generosity throughout his life, even though he was always weak and sickly." "Saint Joseph, the model of the hidden life, helped him to practice the virtues of religious life and to understand better and better the value of suffering and of resignation to God's holy will."

Toward the end of the novitiate year, Brother André anxiously anticipated the day when the superiors of the congregation would decide whether or not to admit him to first profession of vows. There was talk, in fact, of letting him go on account of his weak health, for fear that he might become a burden to the community. In this agonizing uncertainty he begged Saint Joseph for help even more fervently than before and promised him that he would build a shrine to him if he was permitted to make his vows. At that time Bishop Bourget of Montreal was making a visit to the Holy Cross Fathers. Brother André asked for an interview with him, then manifested to him his apprehension and mentioned, among other things, his deep devotion to Saint Joseph, to whom he had made the promise that he would build a shrine to him on the hill opposite the college if he was admitted to first profession. The bishop was moved by this great devotion to Saint Joseph and was glad, because he himself had an unshakable confidence in the foster father of Jesus and likewise planned to build a church in honor of Saint Joseph and to make that the center of a grand place of pilgrimage. He had requested that the Holy Cross Fathers come from Le Mans in France for the purpose of realizing this plan. What a remarkable encounter it was, this meeting between the little lay brother and the bishop, who both had formulated the same plan in honor of Saint Joseph! On the recommendation of the bishop, Brother André received permission to make his profession, and he took his vows on December 28, 1871.

At first he was assigned to be the porter, a modest position, which he occupied for forty years in a small, miserable room among countless deprivations, humiliations, and sufferings. In all that he did, day by day, he allowed himself to be guided by a lively faith and a readiness to make sacrifices. In doing so Brother André became helper and counselor to many students at the college, but principally to the many poor and sick people who made their way to the gate, seeking comfort and advice and help. At his post Brother André developed over the years into a wonderworker who enlisted Saint Joseph as his intercessor and then, trusting in his power, worked marvelous, astonishing cures. It is simply astounding to read about this succession of remarkable answers to prayer and miraculous healings in the biography of the simple lay brother, who accomplished incredible things by his unlimited confidence in the intercessory power of Saint Joseph.

What is most incredible, though, is the way in which Brother André managed to build a shrine to Saint Joseph on Mount Royal, an "oratory" that finally became a magnificent basilica, to which pilgrimages come, year in, year out, to honor Saint Joseph and to ask for his help.

Oratorium of St. Joseph, Montreal

Mount Royal, which rises in the middle of the city to which it gave its name, just opposite the college of the Holy Cross Fathers, was originally a steep hill covered with a dense forest. Step by step, the unassuming lay brother made it into the foundation for the wonderful, splendid shrine that honors Saint Joseph. Brother André was for decades, until his holy death on January 6, 1937, the careful custodian of this magnificent center for devotion to Saint Joseph in the New World. In the magnificent basilica, which is approximately 375 feet long, 230 feet wide, and 350 feet high, the words that the saintly Brother André so often spoke during his life to those who were seeking help can be heard and sensed even now: "Have confidence in Saint Joseph, turn to him in all your concerns!"

Pope John Paul II beatified the humble, pious lay brother André Bessette, the great apostle of devotion to Saint Joseph, on May 23, 1982, and on that occasion said the following in his homily:

Finally, without leaving Canada, we also venerate in Blessed Brother André Bessette a man of prayer and a friend of the poor; but of a completely different kind; a truly astonishing man.

The work of his whole life—his long life of 91 years—was that of "a poor and humble servant": *Pauper servus et humilis*, as was written on his tomb. A manual worker up to the age of twenty-five years, on a farm, in workshops and factories, he then entered the Brotherhood of the Holy Cross, who entrusted to him, for almost forty years, the work of porter in their college in Montreal; and finally for almost thirty years more he remained custodian of the Saint Joseph Oratory near the college.

Where, then, does his unheard-of radiance, his fame among millions of people, come from? A daily crowd of sick, afflicted, poor of all kinds and those who were handicapped or wounded by life found in his presence, in the parlour of the college, at the oratory, a welcoming ear, comfort and faith in God, confidence in the intercession of Saint Joseph, in short, the way of prayer and the sacraments, and with that the hope and often manifest relief of body and soul. Do not the poor today have as much need of such love, of such hope, of such an education in prayer?

But what was it that gave Brother André this ability? God was pleased to give an attraction and a marvellous power to this simple man, who had himself known the misery of being an orphan with twelve brothers and sisters, left without money or education, with mediocre health, in short, deprived of everything except a great faith in God. It is not surprising that he felt himself close to the life of Saint Joseph, the poor and exiled worker, so close to the Saviour, whom Canada and especially the Community of the Holy Cross have always greatly honoured. Brother André had to put up with incomprehension and mockery because of the success of his apostolate. But he remained simple and jovial. Turning to Saint Joseph, in the presence of the Blessed Sacrament, he himself recited, long and ardently, in the name of the sick, the prayer that he taught them. Is not his faith in the power of prayer one of the most precious signs for the men and women of our time, who are tempted to resolve their problems without recourse to God? [2]

[2] "Signs of God's Presence among Men", *L'Osservatore romano*, June 14, 1982, p. 7.

Blessed John of Fiesole, Called Fra Angelico

Dominican Priest, Artist

b. ca. 1395–1400, Viechio di Mugello
d. February 18, 1455, Rome

Beatified October 3, 1982

Cathedral of Orvieto, Chapel of Saint Brizio: L. Signorelli, "History of the Antichrist", detail showing Signorelli's self-portrait (left) beside Fra Angelico.

The saintly friar and painter John of Fiesole, called Fra Angelico,[1] was declared on October 3, 1982, by Pope John Paul II in the apostolic letter *Qui res Christi gerit*[2] to be blessed and so entitled to be honored in the Church's liturgy. On February 18, 1984, he was named, again by Pope John Paul II,[3] the patron of all artists, of painters in particular. This fifteenth-century artist and Dominican priest exhibits a personality that, in the humble simplicity and purity of its priestly way of life in religion and, above all, in the transfigured beauty and deep devotion of the paintings it produced, can enthrall even today.

This artistic friar was born between 1395 and 1400 in Viechio di Mugello and was baptized with the name Guido (Vidolinus). He grew up in Florence, where his sister Checca (Francesca) lived and where, most likely, his entire family had settled.

[1] S. Orlandi, *Beato Angelico* (Florence, 1964); T. M. Centi, "Giovanni da Fiesole", in *Bibliotheca sanctorum* 6:797–805.

[2] *Acta Apostolicae Sedis*, 1983, pp. 796–99.

[3] *Acta Apostolicae Sedis*, 1984, pp. 114–15.

The youth loved to learn, and he looked around enthusiastically in the studios of the Florentine artists, yet he was not drawn at first to a career as an artist but rather to dedicate himself to God in religious life. In 1420 he entered the newly founded friary of the reformed Dominicans of the Strict Observance, San Domenico in Fiesole, above Florence. In Cortona he completed his novitiate, and in Fiesole he made his religious profession before the sainted Dominican superior Father Giovanni Dominici, after having received from him the habit of the order and the religious name of John.

During the Western Schism the Dominicans of Fiesole were banished because of their loyalty to the legitimate pope, and for some time they stayed in Foligno and in Cortona. After finishing his studies and receiving priestly ordination, John of Fiesole returned again to his original friary and was entrusted with various offices there (vicar, prior).

When the Dominicans of Fiesole took over the abandoned Silvestrine monastery of San Marco in Florence as well, John was entrusted with the office of syndicus (steward) there. At the same time, though, he began his artistic activity. He painted the image for the high altar in the church of San Marco and decorated the various rooms of the friary with stirring frescoes. In the cloisters he painted the great cross with Saint Dominic kneeling before it; over the entrance to the sacristy he immortalized the Dominican who gave witness with his blood, Saint Peter the Martyr, who, forefinger at his lips, admonishes the viewer to observe silence; at the foot of the stairs to the dormitory on the upper story of the cloisters he painted the Annunciation, with the inscription: "Virginis intactae cum veneris ante figuram, praetereundo cave, ne sileatur Ave!" [When you come before the image of the Most Pure Virgin, be careful, in passing, not to omit the *Ave*]. Then, as though with flowers from heaven, he ornamented the individual cells, so as to recall to the friars who lived in them the mysteries of the life of Jesus and the blessedness of the saints in heaven.

While Fra Angelico (the "angelic brother", as he was rightly nicknamed) was creating his artistic works in Florence between 1436 and 1445, he also received numerous commissions from various orders (Carthusians, Franciscans, Camaldolese, Vallumbrosians). His artistic activity became more and more intensive, and his reputation ever more distinguished.

When Pope Eugene IV participated in the inaugural ceremonies for the Dominican cloister of San Marco in Florence, he was so moved by the paintings of Fra Angelico that he asked him to come to Rome and do paintings for the basilica of Saint Peter and in the Blessed Sacrament chapel in the Vatican. In 1445 John of Fiesole complied and went to Rome to work in the Vatican. This gave Pope Eugene IV numerous opportunities to admire, not only the artistic talents of the friar, but above all his fidelity to the rule, his obedience, and his humility as well. Therefore he wanted to appoint him to the vacant episcopal see of Florence. The friar, however, described himself as completely unsuited and unworthy of this high office and recommended the prior of San Marco at that time, Antonino Pieroti, who in fact became archbishop of Florence and, as Saint Antoninus, found a place in the liturgical calendar of saints.

Pope Nicholas V, the successor of Eugene IV, also prized very highly the painter-friar "on account of the integrity of his life and his excellent virtues [*ob ejus vitae integritatem et morum excellentiam*]", as Leander Alberti wrote in his work *De viris illustribus Ordinis Praedicatorum* [Illustrious men of the Order of Preachers] (Bologna, 1515). Pope Nicholas V commissioned the religious painter to decorate his private chambers with paintings. This he did, ornamenting them with pictures from the lives of the two deacons, Saints Stephen and Lawrence.

Then in 1446 John of Fiesole worked in the cathedral of Orvieto with his nephew Benozzo Gozzoli. In 1450 he returned to Fiesole, where he had been elected prior.

After 1452 Fra Angelico went to Rome again and took up residence in the Dominican friary at Santa Maria sopra Minerva. There

John of Fiesole (Fra Angelico),
Basilica of Santa Maria sopra Minerva

he died on February 18, 1455, in the prime of life. In the adjoining church he was ceremoniously laid to rest with an inscription on his gravestone that has been attributed to Pope Nicholas V but which probably originated with the Dominican provincial in Rome, Domenico da Corella; it reads: "Hic jacet venerabilis Pictor, Frater Johannes de Florentia Ordinis Praedicatorum 1455. Non mihi sit laudi quod eram velut alter Apelles. Sed quod lucra tuis omnia, Christe, dabam." In so many words it says that Fra Angelico did not seek to be praised by the world as a second Apelles but preferred to be remembered for distributing all his earnings to the poor, with whom Christ identified himself. In another inscription John of Fiesole was called "*verus servulus Dei*" (a true little servant of God) and "*vir sanctitate devotus*" (a man devoted to holiness). In 1516 the Dominican chronicler Alberto di Castello already styled him "*vir sanctus*" (a saintly man). In 1517 John of Fiesole is unequivocally called *"beatus"* (blessed) in the work of Leander Alberti, *De viris illustribus Ordinis Praedicatorum*. From the sixteenth century on there are also images of the painter-friar that depict him with a halo.

At the general chapter of the Dominicans in 1904 in Viterbo, a plan was drawn up to petition the pope for the official beatification of Fra Angelico. This plan, however, was not seriously contemplated until 1955, on the occasion of the five hundredth anniversary of the friar's death. In 1960 the Historical Section of the Congregation for the Sacred Rites made available a *Positio concessionis missae et officii in honorem servi Dei Johannis de Faesulis, qui vulgo dicitur "Beatus Angelicus"*. The year 1982, as noted above, brought the official beatification of Fra Angelico, whose works of art testify eloquently to the friar's love for Jesus and Mary; as G. Vasari wrote in the first biography of Blessed John of Fiesole in 1550, the painter never took up his brush without praying beforehand.

A beautiful tribute was paid to this devout painter-friar by Pope John Paul II in a homily for artists in the Roman basilica Santa Maria sopra Minerva on February 18, 1984:

> "In the presence of the angels I will sing your praise" (Ps 138:1).
>
> During this liturgical meeting, we wish to honour a man who was given the name "Angelico". And his life—in deep harmony with the nickname given him—was one extraordinary "song" to God: "a song of praise in the presence of angels".
>
> With his whole life he sang the glory of God, which he carried like a treasure in the depths of his heart and expressed *in his works of art*. *Fra Angelico* has remained in the memory of the Church and in the history of culture as an extraordinary religious and artist. A spiritual son of St. Dominic, with his brush he expressed his *"summa" of divine mysteries*, as Thomas Aquinas enunciated them with theological language. In his works the colours and shapes "worship at the holy temple of God" [cf. Ps 138:2] and proclaim a special thanksgiving to his name.
>
> The exceptional, mystical fascination of the paintings of Fra Angelico obliges us to pause in enchantment *before his genius,*

which produced them, and to exclaim with the Psalmist: "How good God is to the upright; the Lord, to those who are clean of heart!" (Ps 73:1).

To look at Blessed Angelico is to look at a model of life in which art is revealed as a path which can lead to Christian perfection; he was an exemplary religious and a great artist.

Called "Angelico" because of the goodness of his heart and the beauty of his paintings, Fra Giovanni of Fiesole was a priest-artist who was able to translate the eloquence of the Word of God into colours.

If he drew from his family hearth a clear and strong faith, he received from the Order of Dominicans, which he entered in 1420, a deepened knowledge of sacred doctrine and a stimulus to proclaim the mystery of salvation through the priestly ministry and through painting.

By consecrating himself to God, Blessed Angelico succeeded in becoming more a man, not only with others but for others; his works are a permanent message of living Christianity, and at the same time a deeply human message, founded on the super-human power of religion, by virtue of which every man who lives in contact with God and his mysteries becomes like him in sanctity, in beauty, in blessedness; that is, a man according to the original plans of his Creator (cf. Pius XII, *AAS* 1955, p. 289).

In his own life he made true the organic and essential bond which exists between Christianity and culture, between man and the Gospel. In him, faith became culture and culture became faith lived out. He was a religious who could communicate, through art, the values which are at the basis of the Christian way of life. He was a "prophet of sacred imagery; he could reach the summit of art by drawing inspiration from the mysteries of the faith" (cf. Pius XII, *AAS* 1955, p. 285).

In him art becomes prayer.

By decreeing liturgical honours to Fra Giovanni of Fiesole, I intended to recognize the Christian perfection of the supreme painter, effective and sincere innovator of artistic spirituality, but

I also wanted to attest to the Church's profound interest in the progress of culture and art, and to the fruitful dialogue with it. . . .

Let us turn therefore to *Holy Scripture*, which was the principal source of *inspiration* for Fra Angelico. For that matter, not only for him. For how many artists in the history of culture has this source of inspiration disclosed its truly inexhaustible resources! So it was *in past eras*, and so it is also *in our era*. And every era, drawing from the same source, responds to its inspiration according to ever new approaches, with all the *wealth and diversity of the artistic styles and schools* in literature, painting, sculpture, music and theatre.

To Blessed Angelico the Word of God was, both for his *life* and for his *creative work*, a source of inspiration in whose light he created his works and, at the same time, created especially himself, developing his exceptional natural gifts and corresponding to divine grace. . . .

Let us walk in the direction of this depth pointed out to us by him. And that this may be easy for everyone, especially for the category of artists, accepting the requests made by the Dominican Order, by many bishops and by various artists, *I proclaim* Blessed Angelico Patron before God of artists, especially of painters. To the glory of God.[4]

[4] "Homily at Mass in Honour of Blessed Angelico in Santa Maria Sopra Minerva: Pope Proclaims Fra Angelico Patron of Artists", *L'Osservatore romano*, March 5, 1984, pp. 3–4.

Blessed
Jeanne Jugan

Religious, Foundress

b. *October 25, 1792, Cancale*
d. *August 29, 1879, La Tour
   Saint-Joseph*

Beatified October 3, 1982

Sculpture by F. Maria Bernard

In Jeanne Jugan,[1] the foundress of the Little Sisters of the Poor, a stirring example of humility and of evangelical poverty in the service of the poor was raised to the honors of the altar on October 3, 1982.

Jeanne Jugan was born on October 25, 1792, in the midst of the French Revolution, in the little village of Petites Croix, near Cancale (Ille-et-Vilaine), as the sixth child of a poor fisherman. At the age of only six years she lost her father, who never returned from a fishing expedition at sea. Twice the young girl received marriage proposals. Each time she declined. With regard to a sailor who asked for her hand in 1816, she explained to her mother: "God wants me for himself. He wants me for a work that has not yet been started."

In 1817 Jeanne Jugan began to work in the Hospital Rosais in Saint-Servan, caring for the sick. In this connection she accepted the invitation of a certain Mademoiselle Lecoq to live at her house,

[1] A. Hellau, *Une grande Bretonne, Jeanne Jugan* (Rennes, 1938); P. Milcent, *Jeanne Jugan, humble pour aimer* (Paris, 1978).

not really as a domestic servant but rather as a friend and co-worker. With this pious lady she would call on the sick, day after day, for fifteen years and assist them. During this time Jeanne Jugan became a member of the Third Order of Saint John Eudes in the Society of the Heart of the Admirable Mother (Société du Coeur de la Mère admirable).

After the death of Mademoiselle Lecoq, Jeanne Jugan, together with her friend Françoise Aubert, rented a simple house in Saint-Servan; this served not only as their home, from which they went out to visit poor sick people, but also as a place where they took them in to care for them. The first woman whom they took in—and Jeanne Jugan gave up her own bed for her—was the blind, half-lame Widow Harraux. This laid the cornerstone for the Congregation of the Little Sisters of the Poor, which was founded later. Gradually, as the poor sick people who were cared for in the house were joined by still other poor, old invalids, additional helpers, notably the eighteen-year-old orphan Virginie Trédaniel and her friend Marie Jamet, came also to care for the sick, and, together with Jeanne Jugan and Françoise Aubert, they formed the foundation of the future community of Sisters. So as to provide the necessary support for this little community of Sisters, they began collecting alms. This was to become and remain a characteristic feature of the Little Sisters of the Poor.

In 1842 Jeanne Jugan was elected superior of the little community, which more and more was assuming the form of a religious order. On this occasion two priests stood by her side: namely, the secretary (later the provincial) of the Hospitaller order of Saint John of God, Father Felix Massot, who instilled much of his order's spirituality into the women's community as it was being formed; and the chaplain in Saint-Servan, Father Augustin Le Pailleur, who indeed was a great help to the Sisters but who began to falsify the history of their congregation, in that he eventually presented himself as its founder and allowed himself too much influence over its direction. When Jeanne Jugan was reelected the superior of the small community in 1843, he considered the election invalid and appointed Marie Jamet as superior, though she was only twenty-three years old, whereas Jeanne Jugan, at age fifty-one, was assigned merely to collect alms, and she was prevented from having any part in the direction of the institute she had founded. In 1852 she had to go back to the novitiate house, which was located first in Rennes, then in La Tour Saint-Joseph (Saint-Pern). Here Sister Jeanne Jugan, who after professing vows had taken the religious name Sister Marie of the Cross, was sentenced to apparent inactivity for twenty-seven years, until her death on August 29, 1879. During all these years, however, she was for the novices of the growing congregation of nuns the embodiment of the ideal of the Little Sisters of the Poor and the living rule of this institute.

Jeanne Jugan was endowed with heroic humility; in 1879, when she fell asleep in the Lord, the community of the Little Sisters of the Poor—which had been approved definitively on March 1, 1879, by Pope Leo XIII—numbered 2,400 Sisters in 177 houses, and these were not only in France but had spread beyond into Europe and America.

At the beatification of Sister Jeanne Jugan on October 3, 1982, Pope John Paul II characterized the new blessed in the grand style as follows:

> *Et exultavit humiles!* And he lifted up the lowly! These well-known words of the Magnificat fill my spirit and heart with the feeling of joy since I have just declared the humble foundress of the Little Sisters of the Poor one of the Blessed. . . . [A] close reading of the Position on the virtues of Jeanne Jugan, as well as of recent biographies about her and her epic of evangelical charity, inclines me to say that God could glorify no more humble a servant than her. Dear pilgrims, I have no fears about encouraging you to read or re-read these works which speak so well of the heroic humility of Blessed Jeanne Jugan as well as of that wondrous divine wisdom which so carefully arranges events destined to help a vocation to flower and a new order to blossom, an order which is at once ecclesial and social.

Having said this, I would like to meditate with you and for you on the reality of the spiritual message of the new Blessed Jeanne. Jeanne invites all of us, and I quote here from the Rule of the Little Sisters, "to share in the bliss of spiritual poverty which leads to total abandonment and lifts the soul to God." She invites us to this much more by her life than by those few words of hers which have been recorded and which are so marked with the seal of the Holy Spirit such as these: "It is so beautiful to be poor, to have nothing, to wait simply on the good God." Joyfully aware of her poverty, she depends completely on Divine Providence which she saw in her own life's work and that of others.

Still, this absolute confidence did not make her inactive. With the courage and faith that characterizes the women of her native land, she did not hesitate to beg on behalf of the poor whom she cared for. She saw herself as their sister, their "Little Sister". She wanted to identify with all of the elderly who were often so sickly and even abandoned. Is this not the Gospel in its pure form? (cf. Mt 25:34-41). Is this not the way which the Third Order of St. John Eudes had taught her, " . . . to have one life, one heart, one soul, one will with Jesus," to join together all those whom Jesus singled out, the little ones, and the poor? Thanks to her daily exercises of piety—long periods of silent prayer, participation in the Eucharistic Sacrifice and reception of Holy Communion more frequently than was the custom at that time, thoughtful recitation of the Rosary which she never stopped, and fervently kneeling as she made the Stations of the Cross—the soul of Jeanne was steeped in the mystery of Christ the Redeemer, especially in his passion and his cross. Her name in religion, Sister Mary of the Cross, is a real and moving symbol of this. From her native village of Petites-Croix (in English, Little Crosses—was this a coincidence or a sign?) until her departure from this world on 29 August 1879, this foundress' life can be compared to a long and fruitful Way of the Cross, lived in the joyful peace of the Gospel.

Must we not recall here that four years after the foundation of the Order she was exposed to the abusive and public meddling of some of her first companions? She allowed herself to be stripped of the office of superior, and a little later she went back to the Motherhouse for a retreat which was to last twenty-seven years, without the slightest complaint. Saint John Eudes, her spiritual [father], used to say, "The real measure of sanctity is humility". Speaking to the Little Sisters, she would often say, "Be little, stay little! If we begin to consider ourselves as something, we would no longer be praising God, and we would collapse!" Jeanne really surrendered herself to the spiritual life. In her long retreat at the Tour Saint-Joseph, many novices and Little Sisters came under her decisive influence and she left on her Congregation the stamp of her spirit by the quiet but eloquent radiance of her life.

In our day, pride, the search for success, and the temptation to power all run rampant, and sometimes, unfortunately, even in the Church. They become an obstacle to the coming of the Kingdom of God. This is why the spirituality of Jeanne Jugan can attract followers of Christ and fill their hearts with simplicity and humility, filled with hope and the joy of the Gospel, strengthened by God and by forgetfulness of self. Her spiritual message can lead all those baptized and confirmed to a rediscovery and a practice of that realistic charity which is stunningly effective in the life of a Little Sister, or of a lay person whenever the God of mercy and hope reigns over her completely.

Likewise, Jeanne Jugan has left us an apostolic lesson in reality. You could say that she received the Spirit as a kind of prophetic intuition born of the needs and deep desires of the elderly: their desire to be respected, esteemed and loved; their fear of loneliness and at the same time their wish for independence and intimacy; the sadness of feeling no longer useful; and very often, a desire to deepen their life of faith and to live it all the more. I would even add that, never having read the beautiful words of *Gaudium et Spes*, Jeanne already secretly agreed with what they say about establishing a great human family where all men are treated as brothers (n. 24) sharing the world's goods according to the law of justice (n. 69) which is inseparable from the law of charity. Though the structures of the social security system have done away with much of the misery of Jeanne Jugan's time, still her daughters come across the misery of the elderly in many different countries today. And even where those structures do exist, they often do not provide the kind of home atmosphere the elderly so deeply desire and need for their physical and spiritual well-being. You can see it today: in a world where the number of older people is constantly growing . . . , the timeliness of the apostolic message of Jeanne Jugan cannot be disputed. From the start, the foundress wanted her Congregation not to limit itself to the West of France, but to become a real network of family homes where each person would be received, honoured and even, to the extent possible, brought to a new widening of his or her existence.

The timeliness of the apostolate undertaken by this foundress can be seen from the fact that there are today constant requests to be admitted to these homes and to found new ones. When she died, two thousand four hundred Little Sisters were ministering to the needs of the poor and the aged in ten countries. Today, there are four thousand and four hundred of them in thirty nations and on six continents. The whole Church and society itself must admire and applaud the amazing growth of this little seed of the Gospel, sown in the soil of Brittany, and here, a hundred and fifty years later, so poor in possessions but rich in faith.

May the beatification of their dear Foundress bring to the Little Sisters new strength to be faithful to the charism of their mother. May this event have the effect of drawing more and more young girls throughout the world into the ranks of the Little Sisters. May the glorification of their fellow countrywoman be a vigorous call to the parishioners of Cancale and the whole Diocese of Rennes to the faith and love of the Gospel.

Finally, may this beatification be a source of joyous hope for all the aged of the world, thanks to the great witness of that lady who loved all of them so much in the name of Jesus Christ and of his Church! [2]

[2] "Example of Courage and Humility for Today's World", *L'Osservatore romano*, October 18, 1982, pp. 9–10.

Blessed
Salvatore Lilli, O.F.M.

Franciscan priest

b. June 19, 1853, Cappodocia
d. November 22, 1895,
   Kahramanmaras

Beatified October 3, 1982

On October 3, 1982, the great family of Franciscan religious, which already had so many blesseds and saints, gained in the Italian priest Salvatore Lilli[1] yet another new blessed. He was born on June 19, 1853, in Cappadocia (L'Aquila, Italy) as the son of Vincenzo and Annunziata Lilli. On July 24, 1870, he entered the Franciscan community in Nazzaro (province of Rome), and on August 6, 1871, he made his temporary profession. At that time, however, the Italian government began to suppress all religious orders, and so the young Franciscan went to Palestine in order to complete his studies of philosophy and theology in the Holy Land, to be ordained a priest, and then to work in the Near East as a missionary.

In the house his community maintained in Bethlehem he made great progress, not only in his studies, but also in the spiritual life. After Brother Salvatore took his solemn, perpetual vows on August 6, 1874, he was sent to Jerusalem for further studies. On April 6, 1878, after completing theology studies, he was ordained a priest.

---

[1] G. C. Guzzo, *Vita e martirio dei servi di Dio P. Salvatore Lilli OFM e compagni* (Venice, 1942).

After serving for two years at the Church of the Holy Savior and the Holy Sepulcher in Jerusalem, Father Salvatore was sent to Kahramanmaras in Cilicia, which for the next fifteen years was the field where he labored in his priestly apostolate. The effectiveness of his eloquence brought about in Kahramanmaras a great religious awakening among the diaspora community of Catholics in that Islamic region. It was almost always standing room only in the chapel of the Franciscan Hospice in Kahramanmaras during the Masses and sermons of Father Salvatore Lilli; there was always a long line outside his confessional; the number of communicants increased considerably, even on workdays—so reads a contemporary report about the Armenian mission.

Father Salvatore was also able to accomplish a series of projects that benefitted the mission. He strengthened and deepened relations with the important personages of the region, including non-Catholics and Turks. He built a new chapel, which was solemnly dedicated on October 4, 1893, and he was able to obtain large tracts of land for the mission. When cholera broke out in Kahramanmaras in November 1890, he helped the people who had succumbed to the epidemic and stood by them to support them. He himself did not catch the contagious disease, though he would gladly have died as a "martyr of charity".

In 1894 Father Salvatore was appointed pastor and superior of the Franciscan Hospice in Mujuk-Deresi. This was the locality where the genocidal persecution of the Armenian people was started. Even though Father Salvatore was repeatedly warned by his confreres to flee to safety at some other place, he would always declare, "Where the sheep are, their shepherd must be also." When soldiers whom he had very charitably received nevertheless harassed him and finally wounded him, he only cried out, "Let us imitate Christ!" He said this for himself and for his companions. On November 22, 1895, Father Salvatore was arrested, together with seven other Christians, and brought to Kahramanmaras. On the way there he was ordered several times to give up the Catholic faith if he wanted to save his life. He constantly and energetically

Father Salvatore Lilli, who with seven companions died a martyr

refused. In the end his refusal brought him death. Because he would not bow down and accept the faith of Muhammad, he would have to die. He and his Christian companions were brutally stabbed with bayonets; their bodies were burned.

At the beatification ceremony in Saint Peter's Basilica in Rome, Pope John Paul II said the following about the Franciscan martyr Salvatore Lilli:

It is significant that the beatification of Father Salvatore Lilli, a Franciscan missionary of the Custody of the Holy Land and pastor of Mujuk-Deresi, should take place today, the vigil of the feast of Saint Francis of Assisi.

During the seventh centenary of the death of the Saint of Assisi, in 1926, my predecessor Pius XI wanted to emphasize the union that binds the Seraphic St. Francis to the land of Jesus, beatifying eight Franciscans of the Custody who were killed in Damascus in 1860. Today, during the eighth centenary of the birth of Saint Francis, another son of his, likewise pastorally assigned in the land of the East, is raised to the honours of the altar along with seven martyred parishioners of his.

The history of Blessed Salvatore is simple, but rich in deeds that attest to his great love for God and his brothers and sisters. It culminates with his martyrdom that crowns a life of fidelity to the Franciscan and missionary vocation. Concerning his seven companions in martyrdom we know their names, their families and their backgrounds: they were humble peasants and fervent Christians, coming from a stock that throughout the centuries had preserved whole their fidelity to God and the Church, despite difficult and at times tragic moments.

Among that humble people the young missionary immersed himself with total dedication, achieving in a short time what could seem unthinkable to others. He established three new villages to reunite separated families with a view to better protecting and instructing them. He provided for the acquisition of a vast expanse of land to give work and food to whoever was deprived and tenaciously fostered the instruction of youth. Above all, he set a more intense pace to the religious life of his parishioners, who felt drawn by his example, his piety and his generosity; his favourites were the sick, the poor, and children.

A wise adviser and diligent promoter of social works, he was open to everyone: Catholics, Orthodox, Muhammadans, and to everyone he offered his service with a smile. For this he was particularly loved by his faithful, esteemed and respected by the others.

Then during the cholera epidemic his apostolate glowed with heroic charity; he was at once a priest and a doctor. Heedless of the disease, he went from house to house helping the sick both morally and materially. On this occasion he wrote to his sister, a Trinitarian religious, "I felt such a courage that going among the cholera victims to assist them, administer medicine to them, etc., seemed ordinary things to me". And he indicated the clear reason for this: the priest full of faith in God does not fear dangers and "runs to relieve the unfortunate brother who so many times finds himself abandoned by even his most dear ones" (letter to his sister, Sister Maria Pia, a Trinitarian, 4 December 1890).

When the warning signs of the storm that was coming menacingly near arose with violence, his confreres urged Father Salvatore to repair to safer places. The inhabitants of the area themselves, concerned for the life of their Father, insisted that he save himself. Father Lilli's answer was calm and decided: "I can not abandon my little sheep; I prefer to die with them if necessary" . . . ; and he stayed at his missionary post.

On 19 November 1895 soldiers came into the parish house and the commanding officers immediately gave an alternative: deny Christ or die. Clear and firm was the answer of the priest who for this reason suffered the first outbreak of violence. . . .

Three days later the religious and seven of his parishioners were led away by the troops; they marched for two hours; they were made to stop near a stream, and the colonel offered for the last time the choice between denial and death: "Apart from

Christ I do not recognize anyone", said Father. No less noble was the response of the other martyrs: "Kill us, but we will not deny our religion"; . . .

First to be killed was Blessed Salvatore, pierced by the soldiers' bayonets; immediately afterwards, the other seven suffered the same fate.

This Franciscan missionary and his seven faithful speak with incisive eloquence to the world of today: they are for all of us a salutary reminder of the substance of Christianity. When the circumstances of life make us face fundamental choices between earthly values and eternal values, the eight Blessed Martyrs teach us how to live the Gospel, even in the most difficult situations.

Recognizing Jesus Christ as Master and Redeemer implies accepting fully all the consequences that arise in life from this act of faith. The martyrs, raised today to the honours of the altar, are honoured by imitating their example of strength and love of Christ. Their witness and the grace that helped them are for us a reason for courage and hope; they assure us that it is possible, in the face of the most arduous difficulties, to follow the law of God and overcome obstacles that are met in living it and putting it into practice.[2]

[2] "Example of Courage and Humility for Today's World", *L'Osservatore romano*, October 18, 1982, p. 9.

Blessed
Angela of the Cross
(Guerrero y González)

Foundress, Sisters of the
Cross

b. January 30, 1846, Seville
d. March 2, 1932, Seville

Beatified November 5, 1982

To poor parents who were nevertheless distinguished for their Christian virtues, Francisco Guerrero and Josefina (née González), a daughter, Angela, was born on January 30, 1846, in Seville, and she would become a modern saint of charity. As a child she grew up in religious surroundings and was always lending a hand to her relatives as they did their manual work, especially sewing. In adolescence she proved to be a very eager student, but she also liked to withdraw for prayer and to offer up acts of self-denial and self-control.

Angela Guerrero[1] sensed very strongly even as a youngster that she had a vocation to religious life. She yearned to join the Carmelite order and hoped to do so in 1865. But her spiritual director advised against it and arranged things so that in 1869 she entered the Sisters of Charity. Her frail health, however, very soon forced Angela to leave that community.

Having returned to the world, she became thoroughly involved in works of charity for the poor. With the help of her spiritual

[1] M. Cordillo, *Bajo el standarte de la Cruz. Resumen de la vida de la sierva de Dios sor Angela de la Cruz* (Seville, 1957).

director, Father José Torres Padilla (d. 1878), she founded in 1875 the Congregation of the Sisters of the Cross for the care of the poor and the sick. This institute, approved by the Holy See in 1904, sprang up very quickly and spread with great success.

A humble and at the same time energetic nun, Angela of the Cross, as she was now called, was able to instill in her daughters the spirit of mortification and self-denial and, above all, a great love for the poor. She died on March 2, 1932, in Seville.

Pope John Paul II beatified Angela of the Cross on November 5, 1982, in Seville, and on that occasion gave an extensive homily in which he said the following, among other remarks, about the new blessed:

> In this region of Seville, which is surrounded by the sweet smell of Andalusian farms and fields, I meet the rural people of Spain. I do this while placing before your eyes a humble daughter of this people, who is so close to them because of her origins and her work. It is my desire to leave with you a precious gift by glorifying Sister Angela of the Cross with the title of Blessed while I am with you. We have heard in the reading the words of the prophet Isaiah (58:7–10), who invites us to share our bread with the hungry, to shelter the oppressed, to clothe the naked and not to turn our back on our own, for, "if you bestow your bread on the hungry and satisfy the afflicted, then light shall rise for you in the darkness, and the gloom shall become for you like midday." These words seem to refer directly to Sister Angela of the Cross. . . .
>
> I know that the new Blessed is regarded as the common treasure of all Andalusians, beyond any social, economic, or political division. Her secret, the root from which her exemplary deeds of charity sprang, finds expression in the Gospel reading: "For whoever would save his life will lose it, but whoever loses his life for my sake will find it" (Mt 16:25).
>
> The new Blessed took the name Angela of the Cross, as if to say that she had taken up her cross according to Christ's words,

so as to follow him (cf. Mt 16:24). She understood the wisdom of the Cross in an outstanding way and explained it to her daughters through a concrete image of great expressive power. She imagined that on Mount Calvary beside the crucified Lord another cross stands, "of the same height, not to the right or to the left, but directly opposite and very close." To this empty cross Angela wanted to be nailed with her sisters. She yearned "to be crucified in front of the Lord" through "poverty, self-denial, and humility". United with Christ's sacrifice, Angela of the Cross and her daughters were able to give their testimony of love for the needy. Indeed, the renunciation of worldly goods and detachment from all selfish interests led Sister Angela to that ideal readiness to serve which she defined quite vividly when she described herself as "dispossessed for the benefit of all". Somehow she, like our brother Christ, belonged to others.

The stern, crucified existence of the Sisters of the Cross arises also from their harmony with the mystery of redemption through Jesus Christ. Their goal is not to die of hunger or cold; they want to give witness to the Lord, who died for us and is risen. Thus the Christian mystery is completely accomplished in Sister Angela of the Cross, who seems to be "immersed in Easter joy", in that joy which she has left to her daughters as a testament and which all admire in them. They practice penance by giving up their own conveniences so as to be ready to serve their neighbor: to sacrifice oneself with a smile, without expecting a reward that would diminish the meaning of the sacrifice, requires a firm foundation in the faith.

True to Christ's example of poverty, Sister Angela of the Cross placed her institute at the service of the poorest of the poor, at the service of the outcasts and of the marginalized. She wanted the Society of the Cross to be "in a state of poverty", not merely offering assistance from outside, but helping through a life led under the same conditions experienced by the poor. Sister Angela was certain that she and her daughters belonged to the working class, to the lowly, the needy, "who receive everything as an alms, like beggars". The poverty of the Society of the Cross is not purely contemplative; it serves rather as a dynamic foundation which enables the Sisters to care for workers, for homeless families, for the sick, the poor, for orphaned and uneducated girls, for illiterate women. They seek to give to each person what she needs: money, housing, instruction, clothing, medicine; and everything is always offered with love. The means they make use of are their own work and the alms they beg from those who are able to give. In this way Sister Angela of the Cross created a bond, a bridge between the needy and the mighty, between the poor and the rich. It is obvious that they were not able to put an end to political conflicts and economic injustices. Their task was "the charity of urgency" beyond all divisions, which brings help to the one who needs it at that moment. Her charity was the kind described by the Apostle Paul in the First Letter to the Corinthians: "Love is patient, . . . kind, . . . it is not self-seeking, it is not prone to anger, neither does it brood over injuries. . . . There is no limit to love's forbearance, to its trust, its hope, its power to endure."

By her witness of love of neighbor, Sister Angela of the Cross exercised a beneficent influence that reached far beyond the periphery of the major cities of Spain and spread immediately to the rural areas as well. It could not be otherwise, for during the final decades of the nineteenth century, when Sister Angela founded her institute, efforts at industrialization failed in Andalusia, and consequently the region maintained a predominantly rural way of life. Many men and women moved to the cities seeking secure, good-paying jobs, but without success. Sister Angela herself was the daughter of parents who had come to Seville from a little village in order to settle in the city. Here she worked for several years in a shoe factory. The Society of the Cross, too, consists for the most part of women who come from simple rural people and who have preserved the characteristic traits of their heritage. Their convents are poor but clean, with the furniture typical of modest farmhouses.

During the foundress' lifetime the Sisters opened nine houses in as many localities in the province of Seville, four in the province of Huelva, three in Jaén, two in Málaga, and one in Cadiz. Their work at the city limits took place in families that often had just arrived from the countryside and dwelled in wretched lodgings, without even the means necessary for fighting diseases or obtaining food and clothing for themselves.

Today the rural world of Sister Angela of the Cross has experienced the transformation of a farming society into an industrial society, occasionally with remarkable success. But this attraction of industrial prospects has as its consequence a certain disdain for the land, "to the point where farming people feel that they are social outcasts and the phenomenon of flight from the land into the city accelerates, unfortunately leading to even less humane living conditions", as I wrote in the encyclical *Laborem exercens*, no. 21. . . . To achieve progress here, in the positive sense, it is necessary to apply the spiritual power and the love of Sister Angela of the Cross. May that love, which will never end, be capable of forming the human and religious life of each and every Christian. . . . There stands the figure of the new Blessed, in all her exemplary goodness and closeness to the people. Her example is a lasting proof of that love which shall never end.

Blessed
Maria Gabriella
Sagheddu

Trappist

b. March 17, 1914, Dorgali
d. April 23, 1939, Grottaferrata

Beatified January 25, 1983

A young nun who offered her life to God for the intention of restoring Christian unity through genuine ecumenism, Maria Gabriella Sagheddu[1] was beatified by Pope John Paul II at the conclusion of the Week of Prayer for Christian Unity, on January 25, 1983, in the Roman basilica of Saint Paul outside the Walls.

This blessed was born on March 17, 1914, in Dorgali on Sardinia. Both in her good traits and in those that were less advantageous, she was a true representative of the islanders of Sardinia. On the positive side are loyalty and a sense of duty, pride, and irresistible simplicity; on the negative side, though, are stubbornness, exaggerated self-consciousness, and a bit of violence, which are typical for the Sardinians, and also for Maria Gabriella Sagheddu.

At the age of eighteen she must have experienced a very personal, grace-filled encounter with Christ. From then on, indeed, she devoted herself conspicuously to prayer and to the practice of religion, at the same time performing helpful works of charity that

---

[1] B. Martelet, *Una vita per l'unità dei cristiani: Suor Maria Gabriella* (Rome, 1987).

reflected her understanding that she was rooted in her land and bound up with her family. In a short time she learned now to control the harshness and bitterness of her character. After joining Catholic Action, she worked as a catechist, giving religious instruction to children after school. At the age of twenty-one she decided to consecrate her life completely to God in the cloister of Trappist nuns in Grottaferrata near Rome. Her life from then on was determined by a few essential features: (1) by gratitude for the graces that God had bestowed on her in calling her to consecrate herself to him; (2) by the ardent desire to correspond with God's grace with all of her might and to be scrupulously concerned about bringing to completion what God had begun in her.

What was that, though? The Lord had inspired her to offer up her entire life for the unity of the Church. She felt impelled to do this on the occasion of a week of prayer for Christian unity. This appeal for the reunion of divided Christian communities immediately struck a chord within her: "I feel that the Lord expects that of me." Yet until then she had been completely unacquainted with the problematic divisions among Christians, and moreover she knew nothing about the history of ecumenism. It was only that she was completely ruled by the ardent longing for all people to return to God and for the reign of God to be established in all hearts. For this intention she accepted the daily sacrifices of self-denial, and in this spirit she spent her humble, silent days of Trappist life in work and prayer. "That all may be one, Father!" This was, to a certain extent, her constant ejaculation; the abiding theme of her meditation, though, in the few years of her monastic life that were to follow, was the High-Priestly Prayer of Jesus in John, chapters 17–20.

At the age of twenty-three, on the same day on which she had offered her life to God for the reunion of all Christians, she was stricken by an illness that ruined the good health she had had until then. Fifteen months of this painful illness led to her death on Good Shepherd Sunday, April 23, 1939. "A life dedicated to Christian unity" ended with the petition "that there may be one fold and one shepherd". Pope John Paul II took this prayer as the main theme of his profound discourse during the homily at the beatification of Sister Maria Gabriella Sagheddu.

He spoke first of the three elements that played a decisive role in the conversion of Saint Paul, namely conversion, the cross, and prayer:

> It is great reason for joy to observe that precisely these three facts emerge from the narration in the Acts [of the Apostles]: conversion, the cross, and prayer are essentially the elements on which the movement to restore Christian unity is based. Here at the tomb of the Apostle of the Gentiles, concluding the week of prayer with this ceremony that sees us assembled in a deep bond of charity in the one and same Christ the Saviour, we must together rebuild ourselves with these elements. . . .
>
> In this atmosphere of ecumenical charity we find a perfect place for the brief but so rich story of Blessed Maria Gabriella of Unity, whom I intentionally wanted to raise to the honours of the altar on this date and in this basilica. Her life, first through the Trappist vocation and then through the offering of her life for Christian unity, is totally expressed in these same three essential values: conversion, immolation for the brethren, prayer.
>
> Nor could it have been otherwise. The Second Vatican Ecumenical Council, which in this very basilica and on this same date was announced by my venerated predecessor John XXIII, confirms this. In fact, on the subject of ecumenism, it is expressed in these precise terms: "There can be no ecumenism worthy of the name without a change of heart. For it is from newness of attitudes, from self-denial and unstinted love, that yearnings for unity take their rise and grow toward maturity. We should therefore pray to the divine Spirit for the grace to be genuinely self-denying, humble, gentle in the service of others, and to have an attitude of brotherly generosity toward them. . . . This change of heart and holiness of life, along with public and private prayer for the unity of Christians, should be

regarded as the soul of the whole ecumenical movement, and can rightly be called *spiritual ecumenism*" (Decree on Ecumenism, II, 7 and 8).

For that matter, St. John's whole chapter 17—that chapter whose pages were found yellowed by daily use in Sister Maria Gabriella's small personal Gospel book—is nothing other than the prayer erupting from the priestly heart of Christ, who, in the imminent prospect of the cross, implores conversion of heart for all who would believe in him.

I am happy to note, and to point out particularly to the young people, so fond of athletics and sports, that the young Trappist sister, to whom we attribute today for the first time the title of Blessed, was able to make her own the Apostle's exhortations to the faithful of Corinth (1 Cor 9:24) to "run so as to win", succeeding in the span of a few years—in the stadium of sanctity—to set a number of records that would make the most qualified champions envious. In fact, she is historically the first Blessed to come from the ranks of the Young Girls of Catholic Action; the first among the young men and women of Sardinia; the first among Trappist nuns and monks; the first among workers in the service of unity. Four records set in the arena of that "school of divine service" proposed by the great Patriarch St. Benedict, which evidently is still valid even today after fifteen centuries, if it has been able to produce such examples of virtue in one who was able to accept it and put it into practise "with the mind of love".

In fact, it is precisely in this fidelity to listening that the young Maria Sagheddu—by nature stubborn and sharp, as witnesses and her own holy mother described her—was able to acquire that "conversion of heart" that St. Benedict asks of his children. Conversion of heart that is the true and primary source of unity.

From the moment when the obstinate and impetuous young little girl came in contact with the cross of Christ through the death of her favourite sister, she decided to surrender herself to him, docilely and humbly sought the guidance of a spiritual director, and agreed to involve herself in the life of the parish, joining the Young Girls of Catholic Action, dedicating herself to the youngest children in catechesis, obliging to the elderly, spending hours in prayer. From that moment the "conversion" began that accompanied her day by day, to the point of accepting the call to a vocation and leaving behind, when she was barely twenty-one, the beloved land and her dear ones of Sardinia, to present herself, heeding the voice of her divine Spouse, at the gates of the Trappists.

It is precisely this conversion of hers to God, this need of hers for unity in love, that constitutes the premise and the fertile soil on which the Lord will make descend, at the set time, the call to total giving for the brethren.

The offering of her life for unity, which the Lord inspired in her during the week of prayers on these same days in 1938—forty-five years ago—and which he showed pleased him like a fragrant holocaust of love, is not the start, but the finish of the young athlete's spiritual race. From the union achieved with the voice of God springs the movement of the Spirit to open herself to the brethren.

It is the discovery of the Vertical, of the Absolute of God, that gives meaning and effective urgency to the horizontal opening to the problems of the world. There is here a reminder, valuable today more than ever, against the easy temptation of a horizontal Christianity that would prescind from the search for the Vertex; the temptation of a psychologism that would ignore the mysterious presence and the unpredictable action of grace; the temptation of an activism that would begin and end only on an earthly level and perspective; the temptation of a brotherliness that would refuse to be illumined by a common divine fatherhood.

It is from these premises that the heroic gesture of Sister Maria Gabriella surges to the heights of a great ecclesial event. Precisely because it is born from a sublime conversion directed toward the Father, her opening to the brethren identifies her with the crucified Christ, acquires historic value, and assumes ecumenical importance.

This leads us not only to admire and venerate, but also to reflect, to imitate, to study deeply, to suffer, and above all to pray, in order to root our way to conversion ever more in Christ.

So Blessed Maria Gabriella Sagheddu, who gracefully combines the names of the Angel of the Annunciation and the Virgin of the Acceptance, becomes a sign of the times and a model of that "spiritual ecumenism" of which the Council reminded us. She encourages us to look with optimism—over and above the inevitable difficulties that are ours as human beings—to the marvellous prospects of ecclesial unity, whose progressive verification is linked with the ever deeper desire to be converted to Christ, in order to make active and effective his yearning: *Ut omnes unum sint!* (That all may be one!).

Yes, Lord, may everyone soon succeed in being one. Along with us, she, the new Blessed, . . . asks this of you. *Omnes . . . unum.* Amen! [2]

---

[2] "Conversion, the Cross, and Prayer Necessary for Unity", *L'Osservatore romano*, January 31, 1983, pp. 5–6.

Blessed
Luigi Versiglia

Bishop

b. June 3, 1873, Oliva Gessi
d. February 25, 1930, Li Thau Tseui
Beatified May 15, 1983

Blessed
Callisto Caravario

Missionary

b. June 8, 1903, Cuorgné
d. February 25, 1930, Li Thau Tseui
Beatified May 15, 1983

Two members of the Salesians of Saint John Bosco, a bishop and a young priest[1] who in 1930 suffered martyrdom in China, were beatified on May 15, 1983, by Pope John Paul II. Their life and their death can be an inspiration and an example to the Society of Saint Francis de Sales and to many other Christians besides.

1. *Luigi Versiglia*, born on June 3, 1873, in Oliva Gessi in the province of Pavia (Italy), completed his secondary school studies at the Salesian Oratory in Turin from 1884 to 1888. He studied philosophy and theology at the Pontifical Gregorian University in Rome and in 1893 earned a doctorate in philosophy (Ph.D.). In 1895 he received Holy Orders. At first the young priest was assigned by his superiors to direct the Salesian house in Genzano, near Rome, and to serve as novice master. When his religious congregation sent out its first missionaries in 1906, the exceptionally gifted priest Father Luigi Versiglia was among them. He took over the direction of an orphanage in Macao, which he soon greatly

[1] L. Castano, *Santità Salesiana* (Torino, 1966), pp. 185–217; G. Bosio, "Versiglia, Luigi e Caravario, Callisto", in *Bibliotheca sanctorum* 12:1058–60.

Luigi Versiglia

expanded, according to the Salesian method, to include trade schools, which soon became the marvel of all.

In 1910 Father Versiglia had to flee from Macao because the revolution that had broken out in Portugal had repercussions even in the Portuguese colony in China. Father Versiglia went with his confreres to Hong Kong. At that time the bishop of Macao offered the Salesians the mission in Heung Shan. So for four years Father Versiglia worked as a missionary in this region, making great sacrifices in his zeal for souls. In 1914 the directorship of the orphanage in Macao was transferred back to him. In 1918 responsibility for a large part of the Kwang-Tung region was entrusted to Father Versiglia; the territory became the apostolic vicariate of Shiuchow, which Father Versiglia headed as apostolic vicar. At the same time he was named ordinary of the Titular See of Caristo and consecrated a bishop on January 9, 1921.

The apostolic vicariate of Shiuchow flourished splendidly under Bishop Versiglia: as a result of his strong initiatives, numerous mission stations were established with orphanages and other institutions, with schools, moreover, and seminaries for candidates for the priesthood and the teaching profession. Bishop Versiglia distinguished himself in the virtues required of a Good Shepherd, in magnanimous charity and self-denial and, above all, in his singular courage. Four times he was captured by pirates, yet he always succeeded in convincing them, by his calm, level-headed courage, that it would be better to let him go free instead of killing him. As kind and forbearing as he was toward his opponents, he was severe and stern toward himself. How this exemplary missionary bishop, together with one of his missionaries, namely, Father Callisto Caravario, died a martyr's death is described below in detail. First let us review the major events in the life of the Salesian missionary Father Callisto Caravario:

2. *Callisto Caravario* was born on June 8, 1903, in Cuorgné Canavese into a simple working-class family. When the family moved to Turin in 1908, the young Callisto came into contact with the Salesians while he was still attending primary school. Here the piety that had been imparted to him by his good mother developed further, until it matured into a vocation to the priesthood in the Society of the Salesians. He completed his secondary school studies in the Salesian Oratory at Valdocco and his novitiate at Foglizzo Canavese. He worked then as an assistant to the instructors in the Oratory at Valdocco. Here a great yearning to work in the foreign missions was soon enkindled in his young, enthusiastic heart, so that he requested and obtained permission from his superiors to travel in October 1924 to the Chinese mission of his religious congregation. He was assigned first to Shanghai and Timor, where he also completed his priestly formation. He wanted to become a holy priest, as the deeply moving letters he wrote home to his mother in Italy testify. On May 18, 1929, he was ordained a priest by Bishop Versiglia, his future companion in martyrdom. The young priest was assigned first to Linchow, the mission post that was at the greatest distance from Shiuchow, the seat of the apostolic vicar. Left completely on his own, he was to look after a

Callisto Caravario

Christian community that was only in its beginning stage. In this work he manifested an extraordinary zeal for souls and proved to be a devoted pastor and a selfless apostle.

Only six months had passed since the arrival of Father Callisto in Linchow when he received the happy news that Bishop Versiglia intended to visit the young Christian community in Linchow. Father Callisto traveled to Shiuchow to meet his bishop so as to accompany him from there to Linchow. Their traveling party was joined by three teachers, two of whom were women, and a woman catechist. Together this group boarded the missionaries' boat, which was to take them by river to Linchow.

But early on the boat was attacked by Communist pirates. They beat the bishop and the missionary priest barbarically, because both of them had stood guard in front of the catechist and the women teachers, to protect them from seduction and rape. Bishop Versiglia and Father Caravario were dragged from the boat onto the riverbank and were murdered there out of hatred for the Christian faith, after all the devotional objects and liturgical furnishings the pirates could find on board had been destroyed and burned amid constant derision and mockery. It was February 25, 1930. The

Salesian congregation had lost two able missionaries, but it had gained two powerful intercessors in heaven.

At their beatification on May 15, 1983, in Saint Peter's Square in Rome, Pope John Paul II delivered the following detailed eulogy for the two Salesian martyrs:

1. The Gospel of this Sunday, between Christ's Ascension into heaven and the coming of the Holy Spirit, in its most profound content is well suited to the solemn beatification of the two new martyrs whom the Church presents today for the veneration of the faithful. And the first reading of the Mass, which recalls the sacrifice of the Proto-martyr Stephen, is also well in harmony. Bishop Luigi Versiglia and the young priest Don Callisto Caravario, in fact, are the "proto-martyrs" of the Salesian Congregation, gathered here around the Lord's altar on this joyful occasion. The Congregation's exuberance is that of all the Church, but it is understood that it has an altogether special nature for the Salesian Institute, since this solemn ceremony in some way eloquently seals more than a century's work in the missions on every continent, beginning with Patagonia and the lands of Magellan. Thus there is realized a prophetic view of the founder, St. John Bosco, who, dreaming fondly of the Far East for his sons, foretold marvellous fruits and spoke of "chalices brimming with blood".

Whoever receives the Word of God and keeps it in his heart inevitably becomes the object of the world's hatred (cf. Jn 17:14). Martyrs are those who, in order to remain faithful to this word of eternal life, allow the world's hatred to reach even to the point of taking their earthly lives. They give a particularly living witness to the Lord's saying, according to which he who "loses" his life for him finds it again (cf. Mt 10:39).

2. Martyrdom—it is traditionally said—presumes in the murderers "hatred against the faith". It is because of this that the martyr is killed. And it is true. This hatred against the faith can however be objectively manifested in two different ways: either

because of the very proclamation of the Word of God, or because of a certain moral action which finds its principle and *raison d'être* in faith.

It is always for his witness of faith that the martyr is killed. In the first case, because of an explicit and direct witness; in the second, because of an implicit and indirect, but no less real, witness, rather more complete in a certain sense, inasmuch as it is given in the very fruits of faith, which works of charity are. In this sense, the Apostle James can very properly say: "With my works I will show you my faith" (Jas 2:18).

It therefore follows that murderers demonstrate their hatred for the faith not only when their violence is directed against the explicit proclamation of the faith, as in the case of Stephen, who declares that he "sees an opening in the sky, and the Son of Man standing at God's right hand" (Acts 7:56), but also when that violence is hurled against works of charity towards one's neighbour, works which objectively and truly have their justification and their motive in the faith. They hate whatever flows from faith, showing that they hate that faith which is its source. This is the case of the two Salesian martyrs. The acts of the canonical process arrived at this conclusion.

3. According to the teaching and the example of the Divine Master, martyrdom with which one gives one's life for one's own friends is the sign of the greatest love (cf. Jn 15:13). The words of the Second Vatican Council echo this, inasmuch as they affirm: "By martyrdom a disciple is transformed into an image of his Master, who freely accepted death on behalf of the world's salvation; he perfects that image even to the shedding of blood. The Church therefore considers martyrdom the highest proof of love" (*Lumen Gentium*, no. 42). And this because, as St. Thomas explains (*Summa Theol.* II-II, q. 124, a. 3), with martyrdom one demonstrates that he renounces what we hold most precious, namely, our life, and he accepts what is most repugnant, namely, death, especially if preceded by the pain of torture.

The two Salesian martyrs *gave their lives for the salvation and the moral integrity of their neighbour.* In fact, they placed themselves as shields in defence of three young mission students whom they were accompanying home [or to their catechism classes].

At the price of their blood they defended the responsible choice of chastity made by those young girls, in danger of falling into the hands of those who would not have respected them. A heroic witness therefore in favour of chastity, which still reminds today's society of the very high value and price of this virtue, whose safeguarding, coupled with respect for and the promotion of human life, well merits placing one's life in danger, as we can see and admire in other shining examples in Christian history, from St. Agnes to St. Maria Goretti.

4. The two martyrs' act of supreme love finds its broader significance in the framework of that evangelical ministry which the Church carries out on behalf of the great and noble Chinese people, beginning from the times of Father Matteo Ricci. In fact, in every age and in every place martyrdom is an offering of love for the brethren and especially for the people for whose benefit the martyr offers himself. The blood of the two blesseds is therefore at the foundation of the Chinese Church, as the blood of Peter is at the foundation of the Church of Rome. We must therefore understand the witness of their love and their service as a sign of the profound harmony between the Gospel and the highest values of the culture and spirituality of China. In this witness, the sacrifice offered to God and the gift of self made to the people and to the Church of China cannot be separated.

Christianity, as its millenary history demonstrates right up to the present time, is at ease in all cultures and all civilizations, without identifying itself with any. It finds a spontaneous consonance with all that is valid in them, since both the one and the other have the same divine origin, without the risk of confusion or competition, since they are placed on two different levels: respectively, the level of grace and the level of nature.

The joyful occasion of this rite of beatification arouses and strengthens in us the hope for progress in establishing structures and dialogue, destined to foster this need for harmonization in the Christian people of China between the dimension of social commitment and national conscience, and that of communion with the universal Church: a requirement intrinsic to Christ's message and in conformity with the most profound needs of nations and cultures. Culture, every culture, rises towards Christ, and Christ descends towards every culture. May China too, like every other nation on earth, always better understand this meeting point.

5. But another thought calls our attention. Clearly placed against the background of this tragic and grand episode are two concepts of woman which are irreconcilable: either woman as a person, responsibly striving for the realization of her moral dignity and appropriately aided and protected in this by the human and social environment; and this was the choice of the two martyrs and of the three young women entrusted to them; or woman as an object and instrument of the pleasure and purposes of others. Here, then, is the murderers' choice.

In the Christian Scriptures and Tradition, these two opposing concepts of woman are closely related to the figure of Mary Most Holy, who is, respectively, the faithful embodiment and the total refusal of these two concepts. For some time the two martyrs had shaped their concept of woman and her dignity in the light of the Marian model. Their clash with the aggressors, as sudden and unexpected as it was, therefore found them ready. They died in the light of Mary, whom they had filially honoured and preached their whole lives.

The journey which brought them to sacrifice began with the blessing and under the auspices of Our Lady Help of Christians, Patroness of the Salesian Congregation. The fatal aggression took place at noon, after the group had greeted the Mother of God with the recitation of the *Angelus*. This sweet prayer prepared the victorious battle against the snares of evil. The names of

Jesus, Mary and Joseph rang out loudly from the mouths of the shepherds and the sheep of the flock as soon as the bitter battle presented itself with the enemies of faith and purity, who had no intention of letting their prey escape, not even in the face of a crime.

6. Mons. Versiglia and Don Caravario, following Christ's example, have perfectly embodied the ideal of the evangelical shepherd: a shepherd who is at once a "lamb" (cf. Rev 7:17) who lays down his life for his flock (Jn 10:11), expression of the Father's mercy and tenderness, but at the same time the lamb "who sits on the throne" (Rev 7:17); victorious "lion" (cf. Rev 5:5), courageous fighter for the cause of truth and justice, defender of the weak and the poor, victor over the evil of sin and death.

Therefore today, little more than half a century from their slaughter, the message of the new blesseds is clear and relevant. When the Church proposes some life model for the faithful, it does so also in consideration of the particular pastoral needs of the time in which such proclamation takes place.

Therefore it is our duty to thank above all the Lord who, with the intercession of the new blesseds, gives us a new light and a new comfort in our journey toward sanctity, but also at the same time the proposal to meditate on their example and to imitate it, in proportion to our strength and in relation to our various responsibilities and circumstances. Above all, I am thinking of the Salesian confreres, but a saint's example is always valid for all of the Church. May Christ give us his Spirit that we may succeed in this. May the Most Holy Virgin, Our Lady Help of Christians, maternally help us in these holy resolutions.[2]

[2] "The Blood of Two Missionary Martyrs: The Foundation of Church in China", L'Osservatore romano, May 23, 1983, pp. 1–2.

Blessed Ursula Ledóchowska

Foundress

b. April 17, 1865, Loosdorf
d. May 29, 1939, Rome

Beatified June 20, 1983

The blessed who was beatified on June 20, 1983, by Pope John Paul II in Poznan (Poland), Ursula Julia Maria Ledóchowska,[1] was born on April 17, 1865, in Loosdorf near Melk (Lower Austria), the daughter of Count Anton Walka-Ledóchowski and Countess Josephine Salis-Zizers and the sister of Maria Theresia, who was two years older and later became the blessed foundress of the Sodality of Saint Peter Claver. One year afterward, in 1866, Julia Maria had a little brother, Vladimir, who would later be the saintly superior general of the Jesuits (from 1915 to 1942).

Julia Maria spent the first nine years of her life in Loosdorf. In 1874 the count's family resettled in Sankt Pölten, where Julia Maria together with her sisters Maria Theresia and Fanny received instruction at an English girls' school (Institut der Englischen Fräulein). During this time Julia Maria's spiritual vocation was already taking shape.

Their father, who was ailing at the time, longed increasingly to be in his homeland. So it happened that in 1883 they moved to

---

[1] S. Dal Pozzo, *Una donna polacca da Pietroburgo a Roma* (Brescia, 1949); N. del Re, "Ledóchowska, Giulia Maria Orsola", in *Bibliotheca sanctorum* 12:1058–60.

Poland, specifically to Lipnica in Galicia in the vicinity of Kraków. Count Ledóchowski died there two years later, in 1885, after he had given his blessing to Julia Maria's religious vocation.

On August 18, 1886, Julia Maria entered the Ursuline convent in Kraków and received, with the habit, a religious name, the one belonging to Saint Ursula. On April 28, 1889, she took perpetual vows and was then assigned to educational work, instructing and training young girls. She performed her duties with great apostolic zeal. She established a boarding school for the younger pupils and founded an association of the Children of Mary for the students. Then from 1904 to 1907 Sister Ursula was prioress of the Ursuline convent in Kraków. In this capacity she founded in Saint Petersburg (Leningrad) a boarding school for Polish girls, because she had received a request to do so from the pastor of Saint Catherine's Church, Monsignor Konstantin Budkiewicz. In 1907 Sister Ursula founded an Ursuline convent in Saint Petersburg and another in Sortavala in Finland. She entered into very thoroughgoing ecumenical contacts with the separated brethren there and translated the catechism, as well as a book of religious songs, into Finnish. For the poor fishermen and their families Sister Ursula founded a clinic that helped the sick at no cost.

On account of Sister Ursula's apostolic activity, the Russian press and the Russian police soon were watching her every move; she was pressured and persecuted, and, finally, at the beginning of the First World War, she was expelled from Russia as an Austrian citizen. She fled for asylum to neutral Sweden but was able to keep in contact with her Sisters who had remained in Russia, and she encouraged them to persevere. Once in Protestant Sweden, Sister Ursula soon resumed her contacts with the separated brethren, first and foremost with that great pioneer of ecumenism, the Lutheran archbishop Nathan Söderblom. In her apostolic zeal she cared especially for the Catholics who lived scattered throughout the diaspora, and for them she arranged various opportunities for group retreats and spiritual exercises in common. She also founded a Marian congregation in 1915 and started a monthly Catholic newspaper entitled *Solglimtar*, which, with the title changed to *Katolsk Kyrkotidning*, is still published in Uppsala.

Benedict XV, the "Pope of Peace", appealed to all men of good will, according to their abilities, to come to the aid of the war victims who were in need; Sister Ursula responded with a large-scale charitable campaign for her fellow Poles living in exile. Accordingly she held more than eighty conferences in six different languages in Scandinavia during the war years (1915–1918), at which she spoke about the culture, literature, and history of the Polish people, as well as about their right to freedom, independence, and national autonomy. For the same purpose she founded various local committees that would send donations for material relief to the central committee in Switzerland, which was headed by the great Polish poet Henryk Sienkiewicz (d. 1916). Sister Ursula worked for this cause in Scandinavia with various intellectuals. In 1917 she published in Stockholm the book *Polonica* in three languages. In the same year this uncommonly enterprising and dynamic religious woman went to Denmark in order to care for the Polish emigrants in this country. In 1918 she started a school of home economics and an orphanage for the Polish girls in Aalborg.

After the end of the war, Blessed Ursula Ledóchowska returned in 1920 to Poland, which was again free and independent, intending to rejoin the religious community of her motherhouse in Kraków. Once there, however, she soon noticed that she and the Sisters who had worked abroad with her had distanced themselves, by the very nature of their apostolate during World War I, from the form of community life at the Ursuline convent in Kraków, particularly since their apostolate was no longer directed so much toward girls from well-to-do families but, rather, primarily toward the impoverished, the infirm elderly, and the children of families in reduced circumstances.

Therefore, with the approval of the Holy See in Rome, Ursula Ledóchowska and her Sisters separated themselves from the Polish Ursuline order and founded the autonomous branch of the Ursuline Sisters of the Heart of Jesus in Agony (*Orsoline del Sacro*

Cuore di Gesù Agonizzante; called the Gray Ursulines in Poland). This religious congregation was first approved by the Church probationally in 1923 and definitively soon afterward in 1930. When the seventy-four-year-old foundress died on May 29, 1939, in Rome, the congregation already numbered more than one hundred members in thirty-five convents. Today there are ninety-five foundations in Finland, France, Italy, Poland, Brazil, Canada, and, since 1980, also in Germany.

The spirituality of Sister Ursula and her religious congregation includes a particular devotion to the divine Heart of Jesus in his agony unto death [cf. Mk 14:34]. The Constitutions drawn up by Blessed Ursula Ledóchowska say, significantly, "To proclaim Christ and the love of his Heart is the specific task of our Congregation. We accomplish this through all of those activities that have as their goal the propagation and strengthening of the faith, especially through the education and training of children and youth and through service to the poorest and the oppressed among our brethren." More information about the spirituality of Blessed Ursula Ledóchowska is given in her published writings.[2]

Mother Ursula received a great deal of help in her personal striving for holiness from the influence and example of her sister Maria Theresia Ledóchowska, who was beatified in 1975, and from that of her priest-brother Vladimir Ledóchowski, the twenty-sixth general superior of the Society of Jesus, who led a saintly life and for whom a beatification process is likewise under way.

Pope John Paul II said the following about the new blessed at the beatification ceremony in Poznan [Poland] on June 20, 1984:

On this day I wish in a particular way *to bless the Lord* [cf. Ps 34:1–2], because it has been given to me, with you my dear

---

[2] Ledóchowska, Julia Ursula Maria: Besides the Constitutions and the Directory (Pniewy, 1923–1930), she wrote *Meditations for Sisters*, 4 vols. (Pniewy, 1930–1931); *Meditations for Superiors* (Pniewy, 1932); *The Monthly Retreat* (Pniewy, 1933); *Examination of Conscience for Superiors*; and *Beneath the Star of the Sea*. (The last work has been published in Polish, German, French, and Italian editions.)

compatriots, to be able to raise to the honours of the Altar—by Beatification—the Venerable Servant of God, Mother Ursula Ledóchowska. To the glory of the Beati is raised *a Daughter* of a *famous Polish family*. The locality of Lipnica Murowana (in the Diocese of Tarnow), where the Ledóchowski family has their home, is the same locality from which came, in the fifteenth century, Blessed Szymon of Lipnica. The blood sister of Mother Ursula, Maria Teresa Ledóchowska, commonly known as the "Mother of Black Africa" and foundress of the Sodality of Saint Peter Claver (Claverian Sisters), was beatified a few years ago by Paul VI.

The vocation of Ursula was *youth and the education of youth*, in addition to various forms of help for the pastoral work of the Church. She discovered the path of this vocation in the Convent of the Ursuline Sisters of Kraków. In the year 1907 she left there—with the consent of Pope Pius X—to do *apostolic work* in the city then called Saint Petersburg, in Russia. Forced to leave Russia in 1914, she carried out her apostolate in the Scandinavian countries and at the same time developed a number of activities on behalf of her tormented homeland. When, after the War, she asked Pope Benedict XV to approve *the new Congregation* which had arisen in such an unusual way in the course of this apostolate, she received his approval. The General of the Jesuits at that time, a blood brother of Mother Ursula, Father Vladimir Ledóchowski, was his sister's counsellor at the Apostolic See.

A great influence on the life of the Beatà and her brothers and sisters was their uncle, Cardinal Mieczyslaw Ledóchowski, Primate of Poland and later Prefect of the Sacred Congregation for the Propagation of the Faith. It is known that, precisely here in Poznan, he opposed the policy of the Prussian "Kulturkampf" so as to save the faith, the Polish spirit and the autonomy of the Church in Poland; for this reason he was persecuted and imprisoned.

Here at Pniewy, near Poznan, is the motherhouse of the Congregation of the Ursuline Sisters of the Heart of Jesus in Agony, known as the Gray Ursulines. Mother Ursula Ledóchowska was the foundress of this Polish branch of the Ursulines, and also of the house in Pniewy. The Congregation, however, spread to various parts of Poland and beyond Europe. At the same period, Mother Ursula was carrying out her apostolate (at the request of the Apostolic See) *in Rome*, and she died there, on 29 May 1939. There too is her tomb at the Generalate House in Via del Casaletto.

In numbering Mother Ursula Ledóchowska among the Blessed, we give her to the Church in Poland and to the Congregation of the Ursuline Sisters, *for the glory of God*, for the [*edification*] *of souls* and for their eternal salvation.[3]

[3] "Poznan: Beatification of Ursula Ledóchowska", *L'Osservatore romano*, July 4, 1983, pp. 10–11.

Blessed [Saint] Raphael Kalinowski

Carmelite

b. September 1, 1835, Vilnius
d. November 15, 1907, Wadowice

Beatified June 22, 1983
[Canonized November 17, 1991]

This Polish Carmelite, Jozef Kalinowski,[1] whom Pope John Paul II beatified on June 22, 1983, together with Albert (Adam Hilarius) Chmielowski, was born on September 1, 1835, in Vilnius, the son of Professor Andrew Kalinowski. When he was a student he was noted for his keen intelligence but even more for his piety and great love of prayer. Although he felt drawn to religious life, he began his secondary schooling first at the Institute for Agronomy in Horki, and from there he transferred to the military academy in Saint Petersburg. He left the academy in 1857 with the rank of captain in the engineer corps. In 1858 he became director of the company that built the railroad line from Kursk to Kiev to Odessa. In 1860 he was transferred to the fortress in Brest; two years later he was made colonel of the engineer corps in the general staff of the czarist army. More significantly, during his time in the military Jozef Kalinowski continued to mature as a Christian who lived his faith and took the love of God and the love of neighbor very seri-

---

[1] J. Galfaro, *Al Carmelo attraverso la Siberia* (Rome, 1960); P. Naruszewicz, "Raffaele Giuseppe Kalinowski", in *Bibliotheca sanctorum* 10:1369–70.

ously. He reduced to a minimum his expenditures for his personal needs, for example, in order to help the poor generously, and he founded a Sunday school for youngsters, in which he personally gave instruction as well.

When the popular uprising began in Poland in January 1863, he bid farewell to his military career and fought his way through to the insurrectionists, reaching them in May 1863. He became the commander of the insurrection in Lithuania. He assumed this post only on the condition, though, that he would never have to pass or execute a death sentence. On March 25, 1864, he was apprehended and condemned to death. The death sentence, however, was commuted soon afterward to ten years imprisonment because the Russian authorities were afraid of making a martyr and a saint out of him.

Having escaped death, he now faced, nevertheless, a drawn-out, excruciating ordeal in the prisons and mines of Ussol, Irkutsk, and Perm. He was carted off to Siberia on June 29, 1864. During this time Jozef Kalinowski never complained about his difficult lot but instead was more concerned with comforting and encouraging his companions in suffering by word and example. A strong interior life now matured in his heart. His deep religious sense awakened in him a longing to serve God henceforth—if it would be granted to him to survive—in a strictly cloistered religious order. Finally, he was, in fact, set free in early 1873.

In 1874 he went to Paris. There he was tutor for three years to the Servant of God August Czartoryski. On July 16, 1877, he left France and went to Graz [Austria], where he entered the Carmelite order and began his novitiate. After completing his theology studies in Czerna, he was ordained a priest on January 15, 1882, by Cardinal Dunajewski. In the same year he became the superior of the monastery in Czerna; finally he became provincial definitor of the Carmelite province in Galicia, then superior again in Czerna, and after that in Wadowice, the native town of Pope John Paul II. In 1899 he became provincial vicar, and his efforts helped his order to flourish again. He led the way for his confreres by his constant good example in penitential austerity and prayer. In these spiritual exercises the conversion of Russia was his particular concern.

In 1904, under obedience to his superiors, he began to write his memoirs. Exhausted by so much work and penance and by many illnesses, which he endured in a penitential spirit and with complete resignation to God's will, Father Raphael Kalinowski died in Wadowice on November 15, 1907.

Pope John Paul II gave a homily at the solemn rite of beatification on January 22, 1983; among the many things he said at that time about the Blessed Carmelite Father Raphael Kalinowski were the following:

"Greater love has no man than this, that a man lay down his life for his friends" (Jn 15:13). From [his] earliest years, Father Rafal . . . understood this truth: that love consists in giving one's soul; that in love one has to give one's self; in fact, as Christ said to the Apostles, one must "give one's life".

This giving of one's life for one's friends, for one's compatriots, was evidenced in 1863, through [his] participation in the insurrection. Jozef Kalinowski was then 28 years of age, was an engineer and an officer in the Tsar's army. . . . [He was] inspired by heroic love of the homeland. For his part in the insurrection [he] was sentenced to deportation to Siberia; the death penalty was commuted to "Siberia". . . .

After returning from Siberia, and before entering the novitiate of the Carmelites, Jozef Kalinowski was a teacher of August Czartoryski, one of the first Salesians, himself a candidate for the altars. . . . Father Rafal laid down his life in an austere Carmelite monastery, serving to the end, especially in the confessional, and his contemporaries called him the "martyr of the confessional". . . .

[He is an example] of the admirable evangelical mystery of *kenosis*, of detachment, of renunciation, which opens the door to the fullness of love. Father Rafal wrote to his sister: "God gave himself completely for us, and we must sacrifice ourselves to God". . . . In this way [he was] won by Jesus Christ. In him [he] found the righteousness that comes from God, "becoming like him in his death, that if possible I may attain the resurrection from the dead". In this hope, Father Rafal ended his life within the walls of the Carmelite monastery at Wadowice, my native town, in 1907.[2]

---

[2] "Inexhaustible Power of Christ's Redemption Is Constantly Manifested in Sanctity", *L'Osservatore romano*, July 11, 1983, pp. 9–10. [The homily weaves together the biographies of Blessed Raphael and Blessed Albert Chmielowski (see next chapter) and teaches about their holiness and charity; Prof. Holböck has extracted statements pertaining to each blessed in particular.—TRANS.]

Blessed [Saint] Albert (Adam) Chmielowski

Lay Brother, Founder

b. August 20, 1845, Jagellonia
d. December 25, 1916, Kraków

Beatified June 22, 1983
[Canonized November 1, 1989]

For centuries Saint Francis has not had so admirable a disciple and follower in the love of poverty as the Polish academic painter and founder of a religious order Albert (Adam Hilarius) Chmielowski,[1] whom Pope John Paul II beatified on June 22, 1983, together with the Carmelite Raphael Kalinowski.

This Polish blessed was born on August 20, 1845, in Jagellonia in the Miechów district and lost his father at the age of eight years. When the orphaned boy was eleven he was sent to study at the Cadet Academy in Saint Petersburg (Leningrad). He continued his studies in Warsaw and Pulawy. Everywhere he went, the gifted young man was beloved by his comrades because of his noble spirit, his good heart, and his firm character, but above all for his courage. He proved this when he took part in the Polish insurrection of 1863 against the Russians. He was seriously wounded and lost a leg, but, as a result, he escaped the firing squad.

Adam Chmielowski then went secretly to Paris in 1865; in 1885 he returned to Warsaw. After a two-year stay in his Polish home-

---

[1] M. Winowska, *Frère Albert ou la face aux Outrages* (Paris: Ed. St. Paul, 1953); P. Naruszewicz, "Chmielowski Adamo Ilario", in *Bibliotheca sanctorum* 3:1244–45.

land he went to Paris again, then to Ghent, and finally to Munich, in order to complete his study of painting at the Academy of Arts there.

In 1880 the thirty-five-year-old academic painter entered the Society of Jesus in Stara-Wies but because of poor health could stay there for only six months. What to do now? After a long, interior struggle he discerned at last a call to become an apostle and promoter of the Third Order of Saint Francis, since he had always been enthusiastic about its ideals. In 1881 he started recruiting for the Third Order among the people of rural Podolia, but then after 1884 he continued his campaign in Kraków. It was here that he came to meet Blessed Raphael Jozef Kalinowski. Their conversations about religion awakened in him the determination to give himself completely to God in utter poverty so as to serve the poorest of the poor. As a Franciscan tertiary he wanted to be called from then on by his Third Order name, "Brother Albert". In Kraków he became increasingly well acquainted with the need of the most destitute, the homeless beggars. Alarmed by their plight, which was even more serious on the spiritual than on the material level, he looked after them more and more and put himself completely at their service. He sought to alleviate their need: he practiced such absolute frugality that he himself now lived like a beggar in poverty, and he helped those who shared his fate in whatever way he could.

To start with, in the cold season he arranged to have a heated room where the homeless could warm themselves. With the help of the men and women who began to flock around him, he founded hostels for the poor beggars—indeed, he even established workshops for them where they could earn a little money for their support. Brother Albert, having become a beggar, went on begging for the beggars and provided emergency lodgings for hundreds of these unfortunates and helped them in their physical and spiritual need.

In 1888 Brother Albert, placing his hands in the hands of Cardinal Archbishop Albin Dunajewski of Kraków, professed vows of poverty and chastity and, together with the men and women who had gathered to help him serve the poor, founded the religious congregation of Brothers of the Third Order of Saint Francis, called the Albertine Brothers, and that of the Sisters of the Third Order of St. Francis, called the Albertine Sisters. Before World War II the members of this religious community staffed twenty-four hostels for homeless men and fifty-six hostels for homeless women. Today the Albertine congregation numbers forty brothers who, in eight hostels, carry out Christ's commission: "I was homeless, and you sheltered me!"

Until his final hour, on Christmas day of 1916, Brother Albert lived a poor man, as it appeared, but interiorly he had a wealth of joy and peace in serving the most destitute, the people with whom Christ had fraternized and identified himself. Brother Albert lived entirely in God and in his grace and thereby had a great influence upon everyone he met. "Be good, like the nourishing bread that's ready on the table for all who may be hungry!" That was his motto. So it came about that all people responded to him with sympathy, regardless of whether they were believers or nonbelievers, Christians or Jews. If they were impoverished, he accepted them all, generously and charitably. He put himself aside completely and lived in perfect austerity and self-denial; at his death on Christmas day 1916 he left behind no magnificent work and no great religious family but, nevertheless, the inspiring example of a life that abounded in good deeds.

At the beatification on June 22, 1983, Pope John Paul II spoke of this blessed:

Brother Albert . . . reached [the] heights of holiness . . . by way of love. . . . Adam Chmielowski studied painting and for a number of years engaged in artistic activities before following his vocation, which, after a first attempt in the Society of Jesus, led him to the Third Order Franciscans, from where his Albertine vocation took shape. . . . Brother Albert laid down his life in the service of the very poor and of social outcasts. [He] gave his life

Brother Albert Chmielowski

completely to Christ. And in Christ [he] discovered the fullness of knowledge, of love and of service. . . .

Brother Albert confessed: "I look at Jesus in his Eucharist. Could his love have provided anything more beautiful? If he is bread, let us too become bread . . . let us give ourselves." Brother Albert [did this to the very end, until he] died in his "beggars' refuge" in Kraków in 1916.[2]

---

[2] "Inexhaustible Power of Christ's Redemption Is Constantly Manifested in Sanctity", *L'Osservatore romano*, July 11, 1983, pp. 9–10. See n. 2 in preceding chapter.

On the basis of a new miracle worked by God through the intercession of Blessed Albert Chmielowski (beatified June 22, 1983), Pope John Paul II canonized him only six years later, on November 12, 1989, to the joy of the Polish people and for the consolation of all homeless people, for whom this Polish saint can be a powerful intercessor, just as he was a generous helper to them while on earth.

Pope John Paul II said the following in Polish to the Polish pilgrims in Saint Peter's at the canonization:

And behold Brother Albert: he is a personage who has made a deep impression on the history of Kraków and the Polish people, as well as in the history of salvation. It is necessary to "give one's soul"—this seems to be the leading line of Adam Chmielowski's life, from his earliest years. As a seventeen-year-old student at the school of agriculture, *he took part in the insurrection for the liberation of his country* from the foreign yoke, and he suffered the loss of a leg. He sought the meaning of his vocation *through artistic activity*, leaving works that today are still striking because of their special expressive capacity.

While he was devoting himself ever more intensely to painting, *Christ* made him hear his voice regarding another vocation, and invited him [*to seek something further beyond*]: "Learn from Me . . . I am meek and humble of heart. . . . Learn."

Adam Chmielowski was a disciple ready for every call from his Lord and Master.

The text of the first reading of today's canonization liturgy, taken from the prophet Isaiah, speaks of this decisive call which marked out his road to holiness in Christ: "Release those bound unjustly, untie the thongs of the yoke, set free the oppressed, break every yoke" (Is 58:6). This is the *theology of messianic liberation*, which contains what we are accustomed to calling today the "option for the poor": "Share your bread with the hungry, shelter the oppressed and the homeless; clothe the naked when you see them, and do not turn your back on your own" (Is 58:7).

This is exactly what Brother Albert did. In this tireless, heroic service on behalf of the marginalized and the poor he ultimately found his path. *He found Christ.* He took upon himself Christ's yoke and burden; he did not become merely "one of those who give alms", but *became the brother of those whom he served*, their brother, the "grey brother", as he was called.

Others followed him, the "Grey Brothers" and the "Grey Sisters" for whom today is a great feast. Behold, indeed, the other words of Isaiah's prophecy are fulfilled: "Your vindication shall go before you, *the glory of the Lord shall be your rearguard*. Then you shall call, and the Lord will answer, and you shall cry for help, and he will say, 'Here I am!'" (Is 58:8–9).[3]

---

[3] "These Two Slavic Franciscan Saints Bear Timely Messages for Our Own Day", *L'Osservatore romano*, December 4, 1989, p. 9.

Blessed
Geremia da Valacchia

Capuchin Lay Brother

b. *June 29, 1556, Tzazo*
(Walachia, Romania)
d. *March 5, 1625, Naples*

Beatified October 30, 1983

The Capuchin lay brother Geremia da Valacchia, a native Romanian, was beatified on October 30, 1983, by Pope John Paul II. He was born Jon Kostist[1] on June 29, 1556, in Tzazo in Walachia (Romania) into a Catholic family that remained steadfast in the true faith in the midst of people with other beliefs. At age nineteen, after a happy childhood and an untarnished youth, the young man perceived a calling to religious life. But because of insurmountable difficulties, he wanted to pursue his vocation in Italy, rather than in Romania. On a long, adventuresome journey, via Alba Julia, where he stayed for two years, he arrived then in Bari in southern Italy. He was very disappointed with the inhabitants there, because it seemed to him that they were completely lacking in genuine religious sense. He had reached the point where he was about to turn around and go back to his Romanian homeland, but first he walked on farther to Naples. The lot marked out for him in the field of religion there was a happy one after all, and his experiences per-

---

[1] Teodosio da Voltri, *Jon Kostist, l'uomo che no voleva andare al inferno* (Genoa, 1961); Rodolfo Toso d'Arenzani, "Geremia di Valacchia", in *Bibliotheca sanctorum* 6:215–16.

suaded him to enter the Capuchin friary in that city. On May 8, 1578, he received the religious name of Geremia (Jeremiah) da Valacchia. His entrance into the community turned out well. From the very beginning until his death, the Capuchin lay brother from Romania was, as his first biographer, Father Francesco Severino, wrote in 1670, "a plain, simple, uneducated member of the order who, nevertheless, obeyed the rules at all times and was always content with the humblest, lowliest, and most tiring duties."

Brother Geremia was assigned to work in the Capuchin friaries in Sant'Eframo Vecchio in Naples and in Pozzuoli. Around 1584 he was transferred to Sant'Eframo Nuovo in Naples, where for forty years, with patient, self-sacrificing heroism, he tended and assisted his sick confreres as infirmarian. As time went on, reports of Brother Geremia's sanctity spread beyond the community because in serving the sick he also worked miraculous cures for which there was simply no natural explanation. In carrying out his duties he was noted for the selfless love with which he greeted the poor, especially, who came knocking at the door of the friary, and also the children, whom he loved to instruct in the truths of the faith.

As for Brother Geremia's spirituality, its main characteristic was a very fervent, delicate devotion to our Lady. He lovingly called the Mother of God his *Mammarella*.

When Brother Geremia died a holy death on March 5, 1625, he was deeply mourned by countless people. They instinctively knew, though, that now they had a powerful intercessor in heaven. His body was first laid to rest in the Franciscan church of Sant'Eframo in Naples; later, in 1947, it was brought to the church in Rome dedicated to Saint Lawrence of Brindisi, whence it was returned again in 1961 to Naples, where the relics of this blessed Capuchin lay brother are now interred in the Capuchin church consecrated to the Immaculata in the Piedigrotta section of the city. At the beatification on October 30, 1983, the Pope said:

The Capuchin friar Geremia da Valacchia [is] a son of Romania, the noble nation which carries the imprint of Rome in its language and in its name. The glorification of this faithful Servant of the Lord, after three centuries of mysterious concealment, is reserved to our time, marked by the search for ecumenism and solidarity among peoples on an international level.

Blessed Geremia da Valacchia, by coming to Italy from Romania, re-established a link between East and West in his historical experience, putting up an emblematic bridge between the peoples and between the Christian Churches.

The inexhaustible source of his interior life was prayer, which made him grow daily in love for the Father and for his brethren. He drew inspiration and strength from constant meditation on the Crucified, from intimacy with the Eucharistic Jesus and from a filial devotion to the Mother of God.

He worked generously for the poor, striving with all his means to alleviate their miseries. With enlightened generosity of spirit he said that it was necessary to take inspiration from the liberality of the heavenly Father and to give freely what he had received freely, in order to share it with the brethren in need.

He spent the whole wealth of his generosity and his heroic abnegation in helping the sick. He served tirelessly, reserving for himself, as a longed-for privilege, the lowliest and most wearying chores, choosing to care for the most difficult and most demanding of the ill.

Such an extraordinary charity could not remain hidden within the walls of the monastery. Ecclesiastics, noblemen and common people asked to be visited by the friar from Walachia when they were sick. And it was precisely while going to visit a sick person on a freezing winter day that he contracted double pneumonia, which broke his strong fibre.[2]

---

[2] "John Paul II Proclaimed Blessed Three Witnesses of the Redemption", *L'Osservatore romano*, November 21, 1983, pp. 6–7.

Blessed
Giacomo Cusmano

Physician, Priest

b. March 15, 1834, Palermo
d. March 14, 1888, Palermo

Beatified October 30, 1983

An impressive figure who died on the eve of his fifty-fourth birthday in Palermo, the physician and priest Giacomo Cusmano[1] was beatified by Pope John Paul II on October 30, 1983.

This new Italian blessed was born on March 15, 1834, in Palermo on the island of Sicily. He received his first schooling in his parents' house from a priest-tutor. This probably laid the foundation for his piety, which was then deepened at the Collegio Massimo of the Jesuits in Palermo. Thus the young medical student was armed against the threats to religion and morals during his studies at the university in Palermo.

After Giacomo Cusmano had brilliantly completed a doctorate in medicine and surgery, he practiced the medical profession from 1855 until 1859 with intelligence, skill, and zeal, caring particularly for those poor sick people who could not afford a doctor. Soon he noted that many of his patients from the poorer sections of the city of Palermo were in much greater need of a priestly physician of

---

[1] Pietro Fazio, "Giacomo Cusmano", in *Bibliotheca sanctorum* 4:410.

souls. He began to study theology as well, and on December 22, 1860, he was ordained a priest.

Now both doctor and priest, he felt compelled to start an institution for his poor patients that he called Boccone del Povero (this can only be translated unsatisfactorily as "Bread of the Poor, Food of the Poor"). He began by gathering medicines, foodstuffs, and other material relief for the poor and by distributing these donations to them in their lodgings. Out of this developed a society, which was authorized in 1867 by Archbishop G. B. Naselli of Palermo and was finally approved and blessed by Pope Pius IX.

The physician-priest Father Cusmano wanted to provide his institution with a band of auxiliaries, women and men who would help serve the poor; after twelve years of labor pains, such an association of lay brothers and sisters came into being. On May 13, 1880, the blessed was able to present the habit to the first Sisters; on October 14, 1884, after a long preparation, he conferred the habit upon the first lay Brothers of the Servants of the Poor. On November 21, 1887, Dr. Cusmano erected also the Congregation of Missionary Fathers, who were commissioned to proclaim the Good News to the poor and furthermore to direct and minister to the Servants of the Poor. Then Dr. Cusmano founded additional hostels, hospitals, and orphanages for the poor people in Palermo and in other Sicilian localities. His work soon extended to other regions of Italy, as well as to Africa and to both North and South America.

The ideal that personally motivated this blessed and that he wanted the members of his societies to put into action was "unlimited charity" (la Carità senza limiti). One of his first collaborators, later the archbishop of Palermo, Cardinal Giuseppe Guarino, wrote about Giacomo Cusmano: "God has placed deep within the bosom of this physician and priest the heart of Saint Vincent de Paul. The fervor of his love for the poor was unsurpassable; the integrity of his blameless conduct was truly angelic; the kindness beaming from his face recalled Saint Francis de Sales. I have followed him very attentively through all the stages of his virtuous life, and I must acknowledge: I have never met a priest who was so zealous for the salvation of souls, so amiable and so holy as he."

On February 9, 1888, Giacomo Cusmano said at the inaugural meeting of the committee of the Ladies of Charity—presumably with a view to his approaching death—"My mission is now finished." In fact, he died a few weeks later, on March 14, 1888, in his fifty-fourth year and in the odor of sanctity, lamented and mourned by countless people. The orations that were given at his funeral were very moving; they spoke quite clearly of a saint who had gone home, of an Italian Vincent de Paul.

Pope John Paul II characterized this blessed on October 30, 1983, thus:

To heal the wounds of poverty and misery which were afflicting such a large part of the population because of recurring famines and epidemics, but also because of social inequality, [Blessed Giacomo Cusmano, doctor and priest] chose the way of charity: love for God which was translated into effective love for his brethren and into the gift of himself to the most needy and suffering in a service pushed to the point of heroic sacrifice.

After opening a first "House for the Poor", he began a broader work of social promotion by instituting the "Morsel for the Poor" Association, which was like the mustard seed from which a very vigorous plant sprang up. Making himself poor with the poor, he did not disdain begging in the streets of Palermo, soliciting everyone's charity and collecting food which he then distributed to the innumerable poor who gathered around him.

His work, like all of God's works, encountered difficulties which severely tested his will, but with his immense confidence in God and with his indomitable will power, he overcame every obstacle, giving origin to the Institute of the "Sisters Servants of the Poor" and to the "Congregation of Missionary Servants of the Poor".

He led his spiritual sons and daughters to the practice of charity in fidelity to the evangelical counsels and in striving for holiness. His rules and his spiritual letters are documents of an ascetic wisdom in which strength and gentleness are merged. The central idea was this: "To live in the presence of God and in union with God; to receive everything from God's hands; to do everything out of pure love and the glory of God." [2]

[2] "John Paul II Proclaimed Blessed Three Witnesses of the Redemption", *L'Osservatore romano*, November 21, 1983, p. 6.

Blessed Domenico Iturrate Zubero

Trinitarian

b. May 11, 1901, Dina
d. April 7, 1927, Belmonte

Beatified October 30, 1983

Just as the Jesuits have shining examples to show their candidates for the priesthood in Saints Aloysius of Gonzaga, Stanislaus Kostka, and John Berchmans, while the Passionists have their Saint Gabriel of the Sorrowful Mother; so too the Trinitarians now have a comparable patron in Domenico of the Most Blessed Sacrament,[1] who was beatified on October 30, 1983. There is nothing exceptional by way of outward accomplishments in the short twenty-six years of this new blessed's life story; the one thing that is certain is that he was determined to strive for perfection—and did so heroically—and that he wanted to devote all his strength and ability to becoming a priest according to the Heart of Jesus, so as to glorify the triune God in his religious and priestly life.

What is written in the Book of Wisdom (4:13ff.) can be applied to him: "Consummatus in brevi explevit tempora multa"—"Having become perfect in a short while, he reached the fullness of a long career; for his soul was pleasing to the Lord, therefore he sped him out of the midst of wickedness."

[1] Antonio dell'Assunta, *Cenni Biografici del Servo di Dio P. Domenico del Santissimo Sacramento* (Isola del Liri, 1928).

The son of Simon Iturrate and Maria (née Zubero), born on May 11, 1901, in Dina in the Spanish Basque region, longed for a priestly vocation even as a boy and entered the Trinitarian order at the age of sixteen on December 11, 1917. He began his novitiate in Bien-Aparecida (diocese of Santander), and here he made his temporary profession on September 14, 1918. Then from 1919 to 1926 he studied philosophy and theology at the Pontifical Gregorian University in Rome and earned a doctorate with distinction in both disciplines. He was ordained a priest, but after a short time he came down with a serious illness that speedily sent him to his grave. During his terminal illness he was consumed much more by an ardent love of God than by bodily pains. He died in the odor of sanctity on April 7, 1927, in Belmonte (Cuenca).

Even during his childhood the soul of this future religious was amazingly endowed with a rare charm. As a novice and as a student in Rome he increasingly distinguished himself by his remarkable zeal, his great devotedness to prayer, and his austerity and penitential spirit. He made such wonderful progress in the spiritual life that he decided to bind himself by a vow, which was meant quite seriously, always to do the thing that he thought would please God more. Very soon after the painful death of the young religious priest, the process of beatification was introduced in the dioceses of Vitoria and Cuenca and then in Rome, where it was rather quickly brought to its successful completion. On the basis of the miracles that have occurred through the intercession of this young Trinitarian priest, Pope John Paul II was able to beatify Padre Domenico of the Most Holy Sacrament on October 30, 1983, and said the following about him on that occasion:

> The Trinitarian religious Domenico Iturrate Zubero was born on Spanish soil in the Basque country. His short life of just 26 years contains a rich message which is made concrete in the constant striving for sanctity. There are some special characteristics in this journey which I would like to summarize.
>
> The faithful fulfillment of God's will is an aim which in him

reached very lofty heights, especially during the last years of his life. That is why in 1922 he wrote in his spiritual notes: "Our obedience to God's will must be total, without reserve, and constant". Animated by that spirit and with the authorization of his spiritual director, he vowed to "do always what he will find most perfect", resolving also "never to refuse God our Lord, but to follow his holy inspiration in everything with generosity and joy".

As a Trinitarian religious, he strove to live according to the two central principles of the spirituality of his order: the mystery of the Holy Trinity and the work of the Redemption, which lead to a life of intense charity. And as a priest, he had a clear idea of his identity as "an intermediary between God and men" and as a "representative of Christ the Eternal Priest". And all this enabled him to live each Eucharistic celebration as an act of personal sacrifice in union with the Supreme Victim on behalf of all men.

No less important was the presence of Mary along the spiritual path of the new Blessed, from his birth until his death. His was a devotion which he lived with great intensity and which he always tried to instil in others, convinced that "that path is so good and sure, to go to the Son through the Mother".

Just these few traits place before us the power of an example and of a model still valid today. Through his witness of fidelity to the interior call and his generous answer to that call, Father Domenico indicates to our time a path to follow: that of an ecclesial fidelity which shapes the interior identity and which leads to sanctity.[2]

---

[2] "John Paul II Proclaimed Blessed Three Witnesses of the Redemption", *L'Osservatore romano*, November 21, 1983, pp. 6–7.

Blessed
Mary of Jesus
Crucified
(Baouardy)

Carmelite

*b. January 5, 1846, Abellin
(Palestine)*
d. August 26, 1878, Bethlehem

Beatified November 13, 1983

On November 13, 1983, Pope John Paul II beatified "the little Arab woman Miriam"[1] as "a sign of ecumenical hope and of peace for the Near East". This Carmelite Miriam, who was supernaturally endowed with every conceivable charism and died at the age of thirty-two, is a sign of ecumenical hope because various religions and denominations played a role in her life. Her ancestors were originally from Lebanon and were Uniate Maronite Christians. She was born in Abellin (Cheffa-Amar, Galilee, in a place between Nazareth and Haifa) on January 5, 1846, to Giries Baouardy and Miriam Shahyn—the couple's thirteenth child—and was baptized and confirmed there according to the Melchite rite. As a three-year-old child, Miriam was orphaned; death carried off both her parents, one within only a few days of the other. She was then adopted by a well-situated uncle and, in 1854, at the age of eight, went with him to the vicinity of Alexandria in Egypt.

Just before her thirteenth birthday Miriam was engaged by her

[1] A. Brunot, *Licht vom Tabor: Mirjam, die kleine Araberin* (Stein am Rhein: Christiana-Verlag, 1983); P. Gebhard vom hl. Laurentius, *Mirjam von Abellyn* (Regensburg, 1931).

foster father to a young man according to the custom in the Near East, without consulting her. Everything had been prepared for the wedding in Alexandria when Miriam heard, the night before, the same words that she had once heard in Abellin: "All things pass away. If you give your heart to me, I will always remain with you." The next morning Miriam made it clear to her bridegroom that she wanted nothing to do with marriage, that she wanted to remain a virgin consecrated to the Lord Jesus. In punishment for this she was treated for months like a slave.

When Miriam learned that a former servant of her foster father, a Muslim, was about to travel to Nazareth, she ran to him one evening in the hope that he would take her to Nazareth with him to find her only surviving brother, Paul. The man took Miriam into his home and treated her well at first; finally, though, he insisted that she convert to Islam. "I, a Muslim?! No, never! I am a daughter of the Catholic and apostolic Church of Rome and hope by the grace of God to persevere until death in the only true religion!" This profession of her faith so infuriated the Islamic fanatic that he became violent and slit Miriam's throat. Thinking that the profusely bleeding girl was dead, he wrapped her in a cloth and left her in a dark alley in Alexandria. It was the night from the seventh to the eighth of September 1858. Later, Miriam confided to her spiritual director that she in fact died at that time but was miraculously healed by a beautiful woman dressed in pale blue, who could only have been the Blessed Virgin, and was brought back to life.

The forsaken, homeless thirteen-year-old girl took refuge then in the Church of Saint Katherine in Alexandria, where a Franciscan priest took her into his care and found for her a position with a Christian family as a domestic servant. Several times while in Alexandria, Miriam changed her position for a job more in keeping with her vocation as a consecrated virgin. Eventually she wanted to go back at last to her brother Paul, who lived near Nazareth.

For this purpose she boarded a ship that was leaving Alexandria for Akka. A storm, however, dashed the ship against the cliffs of Jaffa. In Jaffa Miriam sought work again for a few days. Then she wanted to travel farther. Wishing to go up to Jerusalem, she joined a caravan of pilgrims and actually reached the Holy City. There a priest found a servant's position for her again.

From Jerusalem Miriam went then to Beirut, and from Beirut to Marseille, in France. There, in May 1865, she entered the Sisters of Saint Joseph but was dismissed by them while still a postulant because those nuns were of the opinion that, on account of the extraordinary events in her spiritual life, Miriam was better suited for contemplative than for active religious life. Indeed, the extraordinary phenomena that would increasingly fill her later life had already begun quite emphatically. On March 29, 1867, Miriam received for the first time the imprint of the Lord's wounds in her flesh. Finally, together with Sister Veronica of the Passion, her teacher at the convent of the Sisters of Saint Joseph in Marseille, she entered the Carmel of Pau in western France and there, as Sister Mary of Jesus Crucified, she received the Carmelite habit on July 27, 1867.

The restless, nomadic life of this young Carmelite continued when, on August 21, 1870, she traveled to Mangalore in India, where the apostolic vicar Ephrem M. Garrelon, who became her spiritual director, had founded the first Indian cloistered convent. In Mangalore on November 21, 1871, Sister Mary of Jesus Crucified made her solemn profession, taking the vows of poverty, chastity, and obedience. On account of singular extraordinary phenomena, for which there was no natural explanation and which caused her spiritual director, the apostolic vicar Garrelon, to suspect that Miriam was possessed or obsessed by an evil spirit, the young Carmelite was sent back to Pau in France.

Whoever might think that here, at the Carmel in Pau, Sister Mary of Jesus Crucified found rest at last is mistaken. For she experienced not only further supernatural phenomena, such as ecstasies and raptures, but also an impulse, which grew ever stronger, to found a Carmel in Bethlehem. Sister Mary made every effort and applied all her strength to realize this dream. In fact, she was able to return to her home in Palestine in August 1875. The Carmel in

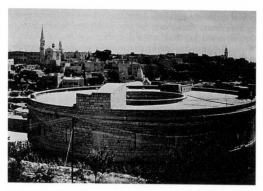

The Carmel of Bethlehem, called "Tower of David",
was founded by Blessed Mary of Jesus Crucified (Baouardy).

Bethlehem was started on September 24, 1875, in a temporary building. On November 21, 1876, it was erected at its final location in Bethlehem, in a convent that was built entirely according to the instructions and directions that had been communicated to Sister Mary of Jesus Crucified. She was already thinking of erecting a Carmel in Nazareth, too. This plan was in fact realized, but only thirty-two years after Sister Mary's death! She died on August 26, 1878, in the Carmel at Bethlehem.

The spiritual life of this Carmelite was full of extraordinary, supernatural occurrences; at the same time, nevertheless, it radiated utter simplicity. Sister Mary was humble and completely unschooled, yet she had a unique gift for counseling others and an astonishing ability to give crystal-clear explanations of theologically deep truths of revelation. She lived in uninterrupted mystical union with Christ, her Bridegroom, in whom she believed unshakably and whom she loved ardently. Besides ecstasies and raptures, she was noted for making prophetic utterances that actually came true. She practiced the theological and moral virtues, above all, humility and obedience, in a heroic manner, and this in spite of the demonic attacks to which she was exposed and which were often persistent. For long periods of time she was privileged to participate in a remarkable way in the sufferings of Christ: from

1867 on she bore the stigmata, which remained visible until she begged the Lord to take this conspicuous grace away from her and to give her in exchange an even greater portion of his bitter pains in his suffering and death on the Cross.

The beatification process for Sister Mary of Jesus Crucified was begun in 1919. In determining whether she had practiced the virtues to a heroic degree, two expert opinions that had been solicited in favor of such a declaration were ultimately decisive: a theological opinion by Father R. Garrigou-Lagrange, O.P., and a psychological opinion by the Salzburg University professor Father A. Mager, O.S.B., dated 1944.

At the beatification on November 13, 1983, in Saint Peter's in Rome, Pope John Paul II said:

> "Hear, O daughter, and see; turn your ear . . ." (Ps 45:11). Today the Church applies these words of the Psalm to Sister Maria of Jesus Crucified, Discalced Carmelite, born in the land which saw the unfolding of the life of Jesus of Nazareth. . . .
>
> "Hear, O daughter". So, in the memory of the People of God, there is deeply inscribed Sister Maria's way towards the *Divine Spouse*. Today the Church crowns her with the act of beatification. This act is intended to give witness to the special spiritual "beauty" of that daughter of the Holy Land; a *beauty* which matured in the glow of the mystery of the Redemption; in the rays of the birth and of the teaching, of the Cross and of the Resurrection of Jesus Christ. . . .
>
> The readings of today's Liturgy [Rom 8:28–32, Ps 45:11ff., Mt 11:25–29] are a splendid comment on the life of Sister Maria, who was born near Nazareth and who died in the Carmel of Bethlehem at the age of thirty-three. Her love for Christ was stern as death: the most painful trials did not weaken her, but on the contrary, purified and strengthened her. And she gave everything for this love.
>
> The entire life of the little Arab, filled with extraordinary mystical gifts, was, in the light of the Holy Spirit, the conscious

and irrevocable reply to a vocation of sanctity, which is to say to that eternal plan of salvation that St. Paul speaks about, which divine mercy has established for each one of us.

Her whole life was the fruit of that supreme evangelical "wisdom" with which God likes to enrich the lowly and the poor to confuse the powerful. Gifted with a great clarity of mind, with a fervent natural intelligence and with poetic imagination characteristic of the Semitic peoples, little Maria did not have the opportunity to pursue higher studies, but thanks to her outstanding virtue, that did not prevent her from being filled with that "knowledge" which has the greatest value and which Christ died on the Cross to give to us: knowledge of the Trinitarian Mystery, such an important perspective in that eastern Christian spirituality in which the little Arab had been educated.

As we read in the Canonical Decree of Beatification, the humble servant of Christ, Maria of Jesus Crucified, belonging by origin, rite, vocation and wanderings to the peoples of the Orient and in some way being their representative, is like a gift made to the universal Church by those who, in the miserable conditions of battle and bloodshed in which they are living, especially now turn with great confidence of heart to her fraternal intercession in the hope that, thanks also to the prayers of the Servant of God, peace and harmony will finally be restored in those lands where "the Word became flesh" (Jn 1:14), he himself being our peace.

Blessed Maria was born in Galilee. For this reason our prayerful thought today wants to go in a special way to the land where Jesus taught love and died so that mankind might be reconciled. . . .

Along with Christ, let us praise the Father because he revealed the mystery of truth and love to the eyes of the soul of Sister Maria of Jesus Crucified and gave her a share in the glory of his Kingdom.[2]

---

[2] "Law of Love and Brotherhood Forms the Basis for International Relations", *L'Osservatore romano*, November 28, 1983, p. 10.

SAINTS

Canonized by Pope John Paul II in the years 1979–1983

Ex Deo nascimur,
In Jesu morimur,
Per Spiritum reviviscimus—
From God we are born,
In Jesus we die,
Through the Holy Spirit we are reborn.

Johann Valentin Andreae (1586–1654)
Lutheran theologian
Preacher at the Court of Stuttgart

Saint
Crispino of Viterbo

Capuchin Lay Brother

b. November 13, 1668, Viterbo
(near Rome)
d. May 19, 1750, Rome

Canonized June 20, 1982

Pietro Fioretti,[1] later the Capuchin lay brother Crispino of Viterbo, whom Pope Pius VII beatified on August 26, 1806, and Pope John Paul II canonized on June 20, 1982, was born to Ubaldo and Marzia Fioretti, a very simple couple who were pious believers and who raised their son to be very devout. Despite frail health he used to subject himself, even in his youth, to severe penances in order to achieve union with God and to lead a life consecrated to God. First, however, he had to earn his bread as a shoemaker's apprentice and journeyman, until at last, at the age of twenty-five, he was able to enter religious life with the Capuchins in Palanzana near Orvieto.

Since he was to become a Capuchin lay brother, Crispino of Viterbo made his profession after a one-year novitiate. Thereupon he was assigned at first as a kitchen helper in the Capuchin friary in Tolfa, near Orvieto, then as gardener and infirmarian. He did his duty everywhere in an exemplary fashion with true Franciscan joy.

[1] I. de Bard, *Das Leben des seligen Bruder Crispinus von Viterbo* (Mainz, 1902); Bonaventura d'Arenzano, "Crispino da Viterbo", in *Bibliotheca sanctorum* 4:312–13.

He spent his last forty years, exhausted and weary from his many strenuous works, his mendicant journeys, and other obligations, in the Capuchin friary in Rome. Here he died at age eighty-one on May 19, 1750.

On his journeys Brother Crispino always combined begging for alms with little catechetical lessons for his benefactors. Although only a modest lay brother, in these instructions he proved to be ingenious and literate; he could quote, for example, entire passages from Tasso's verses about "Gerusalemme liberata". He also composed valuable aphorisms of a religious and moral sort, which have even appeared in print.[2] Otherwise there is not much and nothing earthshaking to report about the life of this simple Capuchin lay brother. And yet there is plenty, because from the numerous anecdotes that began to circulate about this joyful Christian follower of Saint Francis of Assisi, one could compile a whole book of *Fioretti*—which was the saint's family name—just like the *Little Flowers* of the Seraphic Saint.

The remains of this holy Capuchin are preserved in the Capuchin church in Rome, on the left side altar opposite those of the other sainted Capuchin lay brother, Felix of Cantalice ("Fra Deogratias").

Pope John Paul II characterized Saint Crispino of Viterbo at the canonization ceremony on June 20, 1982, in Saint Peter's in Rome in the following manner:

This is a solemn day for us who are invited to contemplate the heavenly glory and unfailing joy of Crispino of Viterbo, counted by the Church among the number of saints, among those who after their earthly pilgrimage have attained the beatific vision of the living God, Father, Son and Holy Spirit, offering us encouraging confirmation of Paul's statement: "The sufferings of this world cannot be compared with the future glory that is to be revealed in us" (Rom 8:18).

[2] *Crispino da Viterbo, Massime e preghiere*, ed. P. Giorgio da Riano (Alba, 1929; Vicenza, 1931).

This is a day of joy especially for the religious of the Franciscan Order of Friars Minor Capuchins, who, while rejoicing for the honour paid to this confrere who hungered and thirsted for justice and was satisfied (cf. Mt 5:6), offer their thanks to the Almighty for his merciful kindness, with which he wanted to give them a new confessor of the faith who, in this year of celebration of the eighth centenary of the birth of St. Francis, joins the other saints of the great family of Capuchins.

In declaring Crispino of Viterbo a saint, decreeing that he be devoutly venerated as such, to the honour of the Most Blessed Trinity and for the growth of Christian life, the Church assures us that the humble religious fought the good fight, kept the faith, persevered in charity, pursuing the crown of justice prepared for him by the Lord (cf. 2 Tim 4:7–8). Truly, Brother Crispino, during his earthly life, stood before the Lord, at his service, and the Lord is now forever his happy inheritance (cf. Deut 10:8–9).

189

In order to follow Jesus Christ, he denied himself, that is, his purely human ideals, and took up his cross, daily tribulations, personal limitations and others', concerned only with imitating the Divine Master, thus saving his life in a perfect and definitive sense (cf. Mt 16:23–25). "What does it profit a man if he gains the whole world and then loses his soul?" (Mt 16:26). The Gospel question just read counsels us and invites us to fix our gaze on that happy goal which is already the possession of our Saint and which is also reserved for us with absolute certainty, in the degree in which we can deny ourselves and follow the Lord, bearing the weight of our day of laborious works.

At this moment may our heartfelt gratitude rise up to God, the Author of Grace, who has led his faithful servant Crispino to the highest evangelical perfection, at the same time imploring through his intercession that we may "unceasingly practise true virtue, for which is promised the blessed peace of heaven" (Opening Prayer).

And now we wish to reflect in a special way on Brother Crispino of Viterbo's message of sanctity.

It was the period of State absolutism, political struggles, new philosophical ideologies, religious unrest (remember Jansenism), progressive departure from the essential contents of Christianity. Mankind in its painful historical travail, in constant search for higher goals of progress and wellbeing, is recurrently tempted by false autonomy, by denial of Gospel values, for which it necessarily needs saints, that is, models who concretely express by their lives the reality of Transcendence, the value of the Revelation and Redemption achieved by Christ.

In the self-sufficient century of luminaries in which he lived, this was precisely the mission of Saint Crispino of Viterbo, the humble Capuchin friar, cook, nurse, gardener, and then for almost forty years a mendicant in Orvieto at the service of his convent. Once again, through divine mercy, the prophetic words of Jesus found eloquent fulfilment in this humble saint: "I bless you, Father, Lord of heaven and earth, because what you have hidden from the learned and the clever, you have revealed to the merest children. Yes, Father, because you have willed it so" (Mt 11:25–26). God accomplishes marvelous things through the work of the humble, the uneducated and the poor, to let it be known that every saving growth, even earthly, is in keeping with a plan of his love.

The first aspect of sanctity that I wish to emphasize in St. Crispino is his joy. His affability was known to all the people of Orvieto and to those who approached him, and the peace of God that surpasses all understanding kept his heart and his thoughts (cf. Phil 4:5-7). His was a Franciscan joy, sustained by a character rich in ability to communicate, and open to poetry, but above all, springing from a great love of the Lord and an invincible trust in his providence. "He who loves God with purity of heart", he used to say, "lives happy and dies content".

A second exemplary attitude is certainly that of his heroic availability to his confreres, as well as to the poor and needy of every category. In fact, for this reason we must say that Brother Crispino's principal commitment while he was humbly begging means of support for his conventual family was to give everyone spiritual and material help, becoming a living expression of charity. Truly incredible is the work accomplished by him in the religious and welfare area for peace, justice and true prosperity. No one escapes his attention, his solicitude, his good heart, and he goes out to meet everyone, drawing on the cleverest resources and also on interventions that appeared in the framework of the extraordinary.

Another special commitment of his holy life was the development of an itinerant catechesis. He was a "lay scholar", who with the means at his disposal cultivated the knowledge of Christian doctrine, not neglecting at the same time to instruct others in the same truth. The time for begging was the time for evangelizing.

He encouraged faith and the practice of religion with simple language, popularly charming, made up of maxims and aphorisms. His wise catechesis very quickly became known and attracted personages of the ecclesiastical and civic world, anxious to avail themselves of his advice. For example, here is one of his enlightening and profound summaries of Christian life: "God's power creates us, his wisdom governs us, his mercy saves us". The maxims overflowed from his heart, anxious to offer with the bread that sustains the body the food that does not perish: the light of faith, the courage of hope, the fire of love.

Finally, I wish to highlight his tender yet vigorous devotion to Mary Most Holy, whom he called "my Lady Mother" and under whose protection he led his life as a Christian and a religious. To the intercession of the Mother of God, Brother Crispino entrusted the entreaties and human problems he met along the street during his begging, and when he was asked to pray for serious cases and situations, he used to say: "Let me speak a little with my Lady Mother and then I'll be back". A simple answer, but totally saturated in Christian wisdom, which demonstrated complete confidence in Mary's motherly care.

The hidden, humble and obedient life of Saint Crispino, rich in works of charity and inspiring wisdom, sends a message for mankind today, just as men of the first half of the seventeenth century awaited the comforting passage of the saints. He, a true son of Francis of Assisi, offers our generation, often drunk on its own success, a lesson of humble and confident adherence to God and to his plans for salvation; a lesson of love for poverty and the poor; of obedience to the Church; of consecration to Mary, the grand sign of divine mercy even in the dark sky of our times, in keeping with the encouraging message coming from her Immaculate Heart for the present generation.

Let us raise our prayer to our Saint who has attained the complete joy of heaven, where there is "neither death, nor mourning, nor worry, because the former things have passed away" (Rev 21:4).[3]

[3] "Humble and Hidden Life of Crispino of Viterbo Carries a Message for All", *L'Osservatore romano*, June 28, 1982, pp. 1–2.

Saint Maximilian Maria Kolbe

Franciscan, Martyr

b. January 7, 1894, Pabianice (Poland)
d. August 14, 1941, Auschwitz

Canonized October 10, 1982

On October 10, 1982, Pope John Paul II began his homily at the solemn rite of canonization of Maximilian Kolbe[1] with the words: " 'Greater love has no man than this, that a man lay down his life for his friends' (Jn 15:13). From today, the Church wishes to give the title of Saint to a man who was enabled to carry out absolutely literally the above words of the Redeemer." But to this Pole with the German name it was given, not only to allow himself to be sacrificed in the concentration camp at Auschwitz in the place of a father of a family; it was also granted to him to love and honor the immaculately conceived Mother of God with such a powerful devotion that one is almost tempted to say here: "Greater love has no man shown to the Immaculata than this Martyr of Love."

On January 7, 1894, in the Polish village of Pabianice, the textile factory worker Julius Kolbe and his wife Maria (née Dabrowska)

[1] F. Holböck, *Geführt von Maria* (Stein am Rhein, 1987), pp. 558–69; E. Piacentini, *Al di là di ogni frontiera: Vita e spiritualità di S. Massimiliano Kolbe* (Città del Vaticano, 1982); Dr. Lisl Gutwenger, *Maximilian Kolbe, Der Heilige der Immaculata* (Stein am Rhein: Christiana-Verlag, 1983).

were blessed with a second son, who at his baptism received the name Raymond.

Together with his older brother, Franciszek, and his younger brother, Jozef, he was raised rather strictly. Raymond was venture-some and enterprising, very lively, and inclined to mischievous pranks. He gave his mother plenty to worry about. She was intent on raising her children for God's glory, yet she could scarcely re-strain Raymond. One day, when he had once again caused her serious trouble, she looked at him sadly and sighed, "Ah, my poor boy, what is to become of you?" The thought seized the ten-year-old and would not let go.

The mother later reported that Raymond "changed all at once". She noticed that he now obeyed as soon as he was told, and it was remarkable how calm and sensible he was becoming. The boy would quite often disappear behind the wardrobe in the room where a little home altar stood with a picture of Our Lady of Czestochowa. One day he tearfully admitted to his mother: "Do you know, Mama, when you asked me the other day what would ever become of me, that made me very sorry, and I prayed to the Mother of God to ask her. Then she appeared to me. In her hands she had two crowns, one white and one red. She looked at me kindly and asked me, 'Which do you want? The white one means that you will preserve your purity; the red, that you will die as a martyr.' So I said to the Blessed Mother: I choose both. Then she smiled and disappeared." He chose both crowns.

Such great love for Mary had probably been instilled in Raymond by his mother. From then on during his whole life he wanted to do everything for Mary and, through her, for her Divine Son and to win all people for her.

Raymond was an intelligent boy, who was interested especially in practical applications of anything technological. At first, though, he was not able to attend school—not because he was in any way unqualified, but for financial reasons; he learned to read and write from his parents. Only Franciszek, the oldest, was supposed to have a chance to study. So as to make this possible financially, Mother

Kolbe took charge of a small grocery store. Since she still served as a midwife as well, Raymond had to help out a lot in the store and also with household chores.

Still, the Mother of God led Raymond by an extraordinary path to an education. One day he had to go to Kotowski, the druggist, who was a friendly gentleman. He was not a little astonished when Raymond told him without a moment's hesitation the Latin name of the medicine he had been sent for. The druggist asked what school Raymond attended. He replied, though, "I don't. I have to stay home and help my parents. But my brother goes to the school and may become a priest. My parents are just too poor to let us both study." The druggist Kotowski then said that he would be willing to give Raymond Latin lessons and to help in other ways, so that not only Franciszek but also Raymond could study.

In 1907 the Franciscans held a parish mission in Pabianice and on this occasion sought to inspire young people to think about religious life. Franciszek and Raymond were accepted into the Franciscan minor seminary in L'viv, the capital of Galicia, a province then belonging to Austria.

In the novitiate, which Raymond began as Brother Maximilian, he was not spared a struggle about the religious and priestly vocations; horrible doubts tortured him. At age seventeen, on September 11, 1911, Brother Maximilian Kolbe took temporary vows. His superiors had discovered his abilities, and so they sent him to study in Rome.

A letter from the beginning of his Roman seminary days that he sent to his mother back home in Poland reveals Brother Maximilian Kolbe's trust in the help of the immaculately conceived Mother of God. He wrote then, among other things:

I was on the point of losing my right thumb. It had developed an abscess that defied medical treatment. The suppuration would not subside. The doctor was talking about amputating the thumb, because the bone was already starting to erode. I told him that I knew a better way. Father Rector at our college had

195

just given me Lourdes water and had told me about his own miraculous cure.

When he was twelve years old he had a diseased foot. The degeneration of the bone had already started to spread. He told me that he would scream in pain, day and night. The doctors considered removing the foot to be the only cure left. After the doctor's visit on the evening before the operation was scheduled, though, his mother stepped in. She removed the bandages, washed the diseased foot with soap and water and then applied a compress she had soaked in Lourdes water. After only a few minutes the boy fell asleep. After a quarter of an hour he awoke again, but completely cured. It was obviously a miracle, but the unbelieving doctor did not want to admit it; he went so far as to devise explanations that convinced no one. After a few days, however, when a piece of purulent bone was discharged through the sole of his patient's foot, the doctor finally had to admit that a higher power had been at work here. He then converted and had a church built at his own expense.

When our doctor here in Rome heard that I had Lourdes water, he said he would be happy to make a bandage with it for me. The next morning the doctor said that there was an improvement, and he probably would not have to amputate the thumb. After a little further treatment my thumb was healed. Glory be to God and to the Immaculata!

On the feast of All Saints in the year 1914 Brother Maximilian Kolbe made his perpetual vows and consecrated his entire life to the Lord Jesus Christ and his immaculately conceived, virginal Mother Mary. The brilliant Brother concluded his studies at the Pontifical Gregorian University (1912–1915) with a doctorate in philosophy and his studies at the St. Bonaventure Theological Faculty (1915–1919) with a doctorate in theology.

More than academic titles, though, he was intent on acquiring true sanctity and an ever more profound appreciation of the exalted dignity of his heavenly Mother, to whom he had consecrated his life. In this regard he admitted later on: "It is an excellent thing to study Mariology, but let us always recall that we become better acquainted with the Immaculata by humble prayer and in the loving experience of everyday life than through wise definitions, argumentation, and subtle distinctions, even though these are not to be looked down on by any means."

In Rome the young religious seminarian came down with tuberculosis of the lungs. No one had given a second thought to his flushed cheeks, his cold hands, and his chilblains because he never complained. After the outbreak of the First World War, though, he began to cough blood occasionally, and, as his condition worsened, he suffered violent hemorrhages of the lungs. Brother Maximilian still remained cheerful through it all and thought that he would soon bid farewell to this world and be united in heaven with the Immaculata whom he loved so dearly. Nevertheless, his sanctity was full of fighting spirit. For example, he could no longer look on while the Freemasons in Rome were perpetrating their mischief to celebrate the second centenary of the founding of their Lodge. Now, full of holy indignation, he wanted to act, and on October 16, 1917—three days after the final appearance of Mary at Fatima—he founded the Militia Immaculatae.

Father Maximilian was ordained a priest on April 28, 1918, in Rome, and then, in the Church of San Andrea delle fratte—where the immaculately conceived Mother of God had appeared to Alphonse Marie Ratisbonne, a Jew—he celebrated his first Holy Mass at the altar of Our Lady of Grace.

In 1935, at the command of his superior, Father Kolbe wrote down a precise account of how the Militia of the Immaculata had originated.

Since Father Guardian now has made it my duty to give a report about the beginnings of the Militia of the Immaculata (M.I.), I want to write down what I still know. I remember how as a little boy I bought a statue of the Madonna for a kopek. At the boarding school in Lemberg [L'viv] I threw myself to the ground during Holy Mass and promised the Mother of God, who is enthroned above the altar as Queen, that I would fight for her. I really didn't know how I should go about it; I was thinking of a battle with real weapons. During the novitiate I took the novice master, Father Dionysius Sowiak, into my confidence and spoke to him about this difficulty. Father Dionysius, who has since died, changed my promise into the obligation to pray daily the prayer "We fly to thy patronage. . . ." I still pray it today, although I now know which battle the Immaculata had in mind. Although I had a strong tendency to pride, the Immaculata brought me more and more under her influence. In my cell I had hanging over my prie-dieu the picture of a saint to whom the Mother of God had appeared. I called on him often. A religious who noticed it said to me, "You must have a great devotion to this saint!"

As the carryings-on of the Freemasons in Rome increased in arrogance and vulgarity—under the windows of the Vatican they unfurled a satanic banner, a horrible distortion that pictured Lucifer casting the Archangel Michael to the ground, and they distributed to the crowds filthy and demeaning pamphlets against the Holy Father—the thought occurred to me of founding an alliance against the Freemasons and other devilish powers. In order to make sure whether this thought came from the Immaculata, I sought counsel from the Jesuit priest Alessandro Basile, who was the confessor of our college. He commanded me, under obedience, to set aside my fears, and I decided to get to work at once. . . .

Besides the first members (Brother Glowinski, Brother Antonio Mansi, and Brother Enrico Granata) no one in the college knew anything about the Militia Immaculatae. Only Father Rector, Stefano Ignudi, was in on the secret, since the M.I. undertook nothing without his permission: in obedience the Immaculata makes known her will. So it happened that, with the permission of Father Rector, on October 17, 1917, there was a meeting of the first seven members. . . .

For a whole year after this first meeting the M.I. made no progress. Even the members were afraid to speak about it. One even tried to convince the others that it was all useless. During this time two from our group, who were truly the elect, went to the Immaculata: Brother Anton Glowinski and, thirteen days later, Brother Antonio Mansi, both carried off by influenza. I myself had a serious relapse and was coughing and spitting blood. Excused from attending lectures, I had the time to write down the program for the Militia Immaculatae that we had worked out, so as to submit a copy to the general of the order, Father Taviani, and ask for his blessing. "Oh, if there were at least twelve of you!" he exclaimed, and gave us his blessing in writing with the request that the Militia Immaculatae be propagated among the youth. From this day on new members continued to join. In the first phase of its existence the Militia Immaculatae had no other duties than to pray and to distribute the Miraculous Medal.

The most important points in the program of the Militia of the Immaculata, which the members or "Knights" were to work and fight for, were: (1) their own sanctification, (2) the conversion of sinners, (3) the reunification of those separated from the Church through heresy or schism, and (4) the battle against the machinations of the Freemasons; all of this under the patronage and with the help of the Immaculata.

Father Maximilian Kolbe attributed the project's turn for the better to the two founders who had died: "They went on to the Immaculata to promote the cause." Afterward, whenever he had to make important decisions, he called on his intercessors in heaven, and he was conscious of their help. He said: "When things threaten to go wrong, the Immaculata calls one of us to herself, so as to help more effectively. Here below we can only work with one hand, because we need the other hand to hold fast to the Immaculata so that we don't fall. In heaven we will have both hands free, and the Mother of God will be our Guardian."

In July 1919 the young priest Father Maximilian Kolbe returned to Poland. According to the doctor's prognosis, his tuberculosis was so far advanced that he was given only three more months to live. The young Franciscan became a professor in Kraków. Filled with holy zeal, he tried to promote the Militia of the Immaculata among his confreres, but he met with little understanding. They called him a dreamer and a visionary. Since his confreres could not be won over to the Militia Immaculatae, he turned to the laity. In the Italian Hall in Kraków he conducted a meeting every month. To begin with there were only a few, but each month more and more showed up to listen and to be caught up in the enthusiasm of the sickly priest, as he explained the four means that the "Knight of the Immaculata" should apply in battling for the Immaculata: good example, prayer, work, and suffering, all for the honor of the Immaculata and in her spirit. He himself set the example, for his personality was radiant with an inner fire that seemed to consume him. He knew that prayer is by far more effective than uninterrupted work, although work, of course, must be done also. He set the highest value on the fourth point, suffering. He said:

> When grace inflames our heart, then it brings about in us a true hunger for suffering, for unlimited suffering, for humiliation and disdain, so that through our suffering we can demonstrate our love to our heavenly Father and our beloved Mother, the Immaculata. For suffering is a school of love. And our activity will be the greater when it is carried out in exterior and interior darkness, when we are sad, weary, and desolate as a result of failure and abandoned by all, despised and mocked like Jesus on the Cross; if we only pray with all our might for our persecutors and desire by all means to lead them through the Immaculata to God. We must not feel hurt if we do not see the fruits of our labor. Maybe it is the will of God that they be harvested only after our death.

Suffering now hit Father Maximilian Kolbe with its full force. At the end of 1919 he had a serious setback with respect to his health.

In January 1920 he was sent to a sanatorium in Zakopane. Yet even here, in his zeal for souls, he gave himself no rest. In December 1920 his superiors allowed him to return to Kraków. Afire with zeal, though he had only half of one lung left, he threw himself into his work again and regularly gave lectures at the meetings of the Knights of the Militia of the Immaculata in the Italian Hall in Kraków.

Since more and more people came, some from a distance, Father Maximilian Kolbe felt a pressing need to publish a small newspaper. He asked his superiors for permission to do so. They consented, on the condition that he raise the necessary funds himself. So he began to beg. That was an extremely difficult sacrifice for him, for he could scarcely bring himself to beg for alms. But the sacrifice was rewarded. Thanks to his mendicant visits from door to door through Kraków, and with the help of the Knights of the Militia of the Immaculata, he was able to collect the money to print the first edition of *Knights of the Immaculata* in January 1922. For the subsequent editions the money for the printer was almost never available, but the Immaculata herself miraculously provided it over and over again. By the year 1924 the circulation of the newspaper had grown to twelve thousand, and in 1925 it reached thirty thousand. Father Maximilian Kolbe, who had to write all the articles for the newspaper himself, used clear, simple language to remind the readers of the most important truths of the faith. First and foremost he promoted true devotion to Mary and, with a subtle understanding of their psychology, prepared his compatriots to make the consecration of their lives to the Immaculata, which indeed was supposed to be the purpose and goal of the Militia of the Immaculata.

Finally they were even able to buy a printing press to print the newspaper. But now the noise caused by the printing and dispatching of the newspaper became too much for Father Kolbe's confreres in the Franciscan friary in Kraków. The old priests were accustomed to a quiet life and could not stand the commotion any more. So Father Maximilian Kolbe was transferred to Grodno, where the friary was large enough. There three rooms could be put at his disposal, one for the print shop, one for the dispatch department, and one for the management of the newspaper. The editor's desk remained in Father Maximilian's cell.

The newspaper was thriving. Eventually still more rooms of the friary were made available for his work, and new machines were procured also. But the director of the whole undertaking had completely worn himself down again. He had to return to Zakopane for another eighteen months in the sanatorium.

On one occasion Father Maximilian Kolbe placed his eyeglasses and his clock at the foot of our Lady's statue and declared: "My glasses stand for my eyes, my thoughts, my work; while the clock stands for the remaining time that I have. It all belongs to her, to her alone; nothing is to belong to me any more. I have given everything to her, she may do with it as she pleases."

A witness testified during the beatification process: "In Father Maximilian Kolbe's life there are two miracles that should suffice to raise him to the honors of the altar: his health—he had only a quarter of his lung capacity left—and his work. Starting from nothing, it kept on developing, defying all reason, and how it became so big was a riddle, even to Father Maximilian himself. In fact, he even boasted of the mystery, knowing full well that the key to it lay in the hand of his Queen."

Meanwhile, the number of novices at the community in Grodno increased considerably. By the time the patient in Zakopane had recuperated and returned to Grodno, the friary there was literally overflowing with the lay brothers who had entered so as to dedicate themselves to the work of Father Maximilian. There was no more room. The only solution was a new foundation.

For that the community first needed land on which to build. A suitable piece of land in the vicinity of Warsaw was advertised to be for sale. There was no money, though, to buy it. In his unbounded confidence in the Immaculata, the friar placed her statue in the middle of the property, silently hoping that the heavenly Mother would help with the purchase. Negotiations began. The provincial found the proposed purchase price much too high and declined. Father Maximilian Kolbe obediently reported to the owner of the property, Prince Drutski-Lubetski, that the community was not in a position to buy the building site. "What will happen to the statue, then?" the prince asked. Father Maximilian's answer: "It can stay there." The prince thought for a moment. Then he said, "Well, in that case, take the property; you can have it for free." Now the provincial approved, too. In the machine room of the friary in Grodno, though, Father Maximilian asked his co-workers, "Get on your knees, my sons, we're going to thank the dear Blessed Mother."

Now work began on the building site. Many people from the area volunteered their help. On the feast of the Presentation of the Blessed Virgin Mary in 1927, construction had progressed to where the Brothers could leave the friary in Grodno and move into barracks in the newly built city of the Immaculata, Niepokalanów. From that day on, when the Brothers had the chance to work for their city, their heroism knew no bounds. One building after another went up, until the complex looked like a little industrial city. The circulation of the newspaper *Knights of the Immaculata* increased from one year to the next, until in 1939 the number of subscribers reached one million. In Niepokalanów, just before the invasion of the German Wehrmacht, the workforce consisted of six priests and more than seven hundred Brothers.

The driving force behind all this was Father Maximilian Kolbe, with his boundless love for the Immaculata. He explained it this way in one of his written works:

Maria Immaculata: the Immaculate Conception is our ideal. If we draw close to her, we will become more and more like her. Let us allow her to take possession of our hearts and of our whole being, so that she can live and work in us and so that she can love God through us with our hearts; for we belong to her completely and absolutely, she is our ideal. Let us apply ourselves, right where we are, to winning other people for her, so that the hearts of our fellow men, too, will be open to her, so that she can reign in the hearts of all people, whatever corner of the world they may live in, without distinction as to race, nationality, or language, and so too in the hearts of all, at whatever moment in history they will live, until the end of the ages; she is our ideal.

Since Father Maximilian's work in Niepokalanów was thriving, he received permission to develop a similar project in Japan. He traveled there in 1930 with four Brothers. On April 24, 1930, he arrived in Nagasaki. On May 24, 1930—precisely one month after their arrival—Father Maximilian Kolbe sent a telegram to Niepokalanów: "We are sending out today the first edition in Japanese. Long live the Immaculata!" The impossible had happened: the zealous, apostolic priest had won over the Japanese people by his evident humility, simplicity, and poverty, by his prayers and sacrifices. He quickly found co-workers, among them Protestants, too. Thus the first translator of his articles, which he wrote in Latin or Italian, was a Methodist.

Indefatigably Father Maximilian toiled on, despite miserable health, and even devised new plans: "As soon as our newspaper is firmly anchored here in Japan, I want to found one in India and after that another in Beirut for the Arabs. I will publish them in Turkish, Hebrew, and Arabic, also. The campaign of our Militia must reach a billion readers! Half of humanity!" In Japan they were soon printing ten thousand copies of each issue.

After this success he was called to L'viv for the provincial chapter of his community. He traveled home with a heavy heart, because it was likely that his work in Japan would now be questioned. But he obeyed. He had done what was within his power. The Immaculata's turn had come now! And so it happened: in L'viv he received all the necessary authority and was permitted to return to Japan. This time he rode through Russia to Japan and stayed for a short time in Moscow. His ardent desire was to publish his newspaper in Russian as well. Shortly before his martyrdom he ceremoniously declared in the presence of several witnesses: "One day you will see the statue of the Immaculata placed on the highest pinnacle of the Kremlin. Before this happens, though, we must undergo a bloody trial."

In Nagasaki Father Maximilian Kolbe bought a building site at the edge of the city. People shook their heads, because he perched his new construction for the Japanese Niepokalanów, for the "Garden of the Immaculata", on the side of a mountain. Only after the atom bomb hit Nagasaki on August 9, 1945, did they understand Father Maximilian's decision. Whereas the city with its 241,000 inhabitants had been almost leveled to the ground, in the Garden of the Immaculata only the windowpanes were shattered; no lives were lost.

After a difficult but ultimately successful attempt to transplant his work to India as well, Father Maximilian Kolbe returned to Japan, where many were joining the Militia of the Immaculata and many others were converting to Christianity. In 1936, though, Father Maximilian was called home again for the provincial chapter and was elected Guardian (superior) of Niepokalanów. He quietly obeyed, for "through the mouth of my superior speaks the Immaculata."

In his homeland the Franciscan priest went to work with ardent zeal for the cause of the Immaculata. He had a premonition, though, that a terrible persecution was about to overtake him and the work of the Immaculata; therefore, he wanted to make use of every last minute.

On September 19, 1939, Father Maximilian Kolbe, together with [some of] his confreres, was apprehended by the Gestapo and deported, first, to Lamsdorf in Germany and, from there, to the camp at Amtlitz. After about three months he was allowed to return to Niepokalanów, where he immediately resumed his duties. In 1941 he and four confreres were once again arrested by the Gestapo and handed over to the authorities at the dreaded Pawiak Prison in Warsaw. On May 28, 1941, he was deported from there to Auschwitz and, together with other priests, was sentenced to hard labor in Block 17. A little later he was put into the block for those unable to work, since he was utterly exhausted by constant waves of fever.

He ended up in Block 14, which housed those who were employed doing less strenuous work.

On one July evening in 1941 a prisoner managed to escape from Block 14. Since the fugitive could not be captured, ten prisoners were selected for execution, as was the usual procedure in the concentration camp. Among them was a certain Franz Gajowniczek, who in his despair repeated over and over the names of his wife and children. Father Kolbe stepped out of formation and addressed Kommandant Fritsch, the camp commander: "I am a Polish Catholic priest. I would like to take the place of this man, since he has a wife and children." The exchange was approved. With the other nine condemned prisoners, Father Maximilian was locked into the death bunker. Here he consoled and encouraged his companions in suffering and prepared them for death.

On August 14, 1941, on the eve of the feast of the Assumption of the Blessed Virgin Mary into heaven, a medic entered the death bunker to administer a lethal injection to the last four surviving prisoners. Father Kolbe was the last of the ten to die. According to the testimony of a prisoner who was commanded to dispose of the bodies, Father Maximilian held out his arm for the deadly injection with a peaceful, radiant expression on his face. His body—like those of the other dead men—was reduced to ashes in the crematorium of Auschwitz.

During the Solemn Mass at the canonization of Father Maximilian Maria Kolbe in Saint Peter's Square in Rome on October 10, 1982, Pope John Paul II, after the introductory words quoted earlier, said the following in his homily:

> Towards the end of July 1941, when the camp commandant ordered the prisoners destined to die of starvation to be lined up, this man, *Maximilian Maria Kolbe*, offered himself spontaneously, and said that he was ready to go to death in the place of one of them. This readiness was accepted, and after more than two weeks of torment caused by starvation, Father Maximilian's life was ended with a lethal injection, on 14 August 1941. . . .

Father Maximilian Kolbe, himself being a prisoner of the concentration camp, defended, in that place of death, the right to life of an innocent man. . . . This man (Franciszek Gajowniczek) is still living and is here among us. . . .

Maximilian prepared for this definitive sacrifice by following Christ from the first years of his life in Poland. From those years comes the mysterious dream of two crowns: one white and one red, [between] which our saint does not choose, but accepts them both. From the years of his youth, in fact, he was filled with a great *love of Christ* and *desire for martyrdom*.

This love and this desire accompanied him along the path of his Franciscan and priestly vocation, for which he prepared himself both in Poland and in Rome. This love and this desire followed him through all the places of his priestly and Franciscan service in Poland, and also of his missionary service in Japan.

The inspiration of his whole life was *the Immaculate Virgin*, to whom he entrusted his love for Christ and his desire for martyrdom. In the mystery of the Immaculate Conception there revealed itself before the eyes of his soul that marvellous and supernatural *world of God's grace* offered to man. The faith and works of the whole life of Father Maximilian show that he thought of his cooperation with divine grace as a soldierly service under the banner *of the Immaculate Conception*. *The Marian characteristic* is particularly expressive in the life and holiness of Father Kolbe. His whole apostolate, both in his homeland and on the missions, was similarly marked with this sign. Both in Poland and in Japan, the centres of this apostolate were the special cities of the Immaculata ("Niepokalanów" in Poland, "Mugenzai no Sono" in Japan).

What happened in the starvation bunker in the concentration camp at Oswiecim (Auschwitz) on 14 August 1941? . . . Maximilian did not die, but "gave his life . . . for his brother". In that death, terrible from the human point of view, there was the whole definitive *greatness of the human act* and of the human choice: he spontaneously offered himself up to death out of love.

And in this human death of his there was the clear *witness* borne to Christ: the witness *borne in Christ* to the dignity of man, to the sanctity of his life and to the saving power of death, in which the power of love is made manifest. Precisely for this reason the death of Maximilian Kolbe became a *sign of victory*. This was victory won over all the system of contempt and hate for man and for what is divine in man, a victory like that won by our Lord Jesus Christ *on Calvary.* . . .

The Church accepts this sign of victory, won through the power of Christ's Redemption, with reverence and gratitude. She seeks to discern its eloquence with all humility and love.

As ever, when the Church proclaims the holiness of her sons and daughters, as also in the present case, she seeks to act with all due exactness and responsibility, searching into all the aspects of the life and death of the Servant of God. . . .

And so, in judging the cause of Blessed Maximilian Kolbe—even after his Beatification—it was necessary to take into consideration many voices of the People of God, and especially of our Brothers in the episcopate; both in Poland and also in Germany, who asked that Maximilian Kolbe be proclaimed *as a martyr* saint. . . .

Does not this death, faced spontaneously, for love of man, constitute a particular fulfilment of the words of Christ? Does not this death make Maximilian *particularly like to Christ*, the Model of all Martyrs, who gives his own life on the Cross for his brethren? Does not such a death possess a particular and penetrating *eloquence for our age*?

Does not this death constitute a *particularly authentic witness* of the Church in the modern world?

And so, in virtue of my apostolic authority I have decreed that Maximilian Maria Kolbe, who after his Beatification was venerated as a Confessor, shall henceforward be venerated *also as a Martyr*![2]

[2] "He Died a Martyr of Love, Giving His Life for Another", *L'Osservatore romano*, October 18, 1982, pp. 1, 12.

Saint Marguerite Bourgeoys

Foundress of the
Congregation of Notre
Dame of Montreal

b. April 17, 1620, Troyes (France)
d. January 12, 1700, Montreal

Canonized October 31, 1982

Sincere devotion to Mary, both in individuals and in nations and peoples, is a barometer of a true Christian spirit—ever since the God-Man Jesus Christ himself loved and honored Mary as his Mother—and so it seems that God raises up souls, time and again, in whose conduct and lives he wills to make it especially clear that a childlike love and respect for Mary is the pathway to Christ that is best suited to our condition, while being also the quickest, safest, and easiest way to God. To these souls evidently belongs Marguerite Bourgeoys,[1] who was born in Troyes in France on April 17, 1620, as the third of nine children of a tradesman, and who at the age of thirty-three went to Canada (then called "New France") and founded there the Congregation of Notre Dame of Montreal.

At the age of eighteen Marguerite lost her mother and so had to devote herself to keeping house in her place and caring for her younger brothers and sisters. She had developed into quite a beautiful young woman and was very gifted. This inclined her to vanity and awakened in her a worldly spirit. She was in serious danger of straying from the right path. But then the Virgin Mother of God in a remarkable way showed her maternal care for the twenty-year-old girl. On the first Sunday in October 1640, in

---

[1] G. Della Cioppa, *La Beata Margherita Bourgeoys* (Rome, 1950).

Troyes, a procession was held in honor of the Queen of the Holy Rosary. Marguerite took part in it. As she walked by the church, her glance fell on the statue of the Blessed Mother that stood over the entrance to the church. The image of Mary, which Marguerite had often seen before, seemed to her on this occasion to be remarkably bright and beautiful. This time the sight captivated her and literally transformed her, so that she later wrote about it as a decisive experience in her life: "As I looked I was touched and changed to such an extent that I did not recognize myself any more. . . . And my transformation became apparent to all. Everyone knew that until then I was irresponsible, funny, cheerful, and a joker, and that my girlfriends just had to put up with me. But from that moment on I gave up my amusements and withdrew from the world so as to devote myself completely to the service of God."

The Augustinian Canonesses Regular of Our Lady, founded in 1597 by Saint Peter Fourier (d. 1640), would have been glad to admit Marguerite. For several reasons she did not apply to that community but instead joined a kind of Marian association for laywomen and became its prefect. For twelve years she held this office to the satisfaction of everyone. Then her confessor, the Carmelite Father Gendret, advised her to enter a contemplative order. She was turned away, however, by both the Carmelites and the Poor Clares. Father Gendret then thought of founding a community, with the help of his directee Marguerite Bourgeoys, in which the interior life of Mary would be particularly honored and imitated. Marguerite was willing to try, because ever since her transformation her goal had been to make the Blessed Virgin's way of thinking her own. Of the three companions who were going to start this proposed foundation, however, one died very soon afterward and another withdrew. This left only Marguerite, who was still not completely free herself, because she felt obliged to care for her sick father until his death.

Meanwhile, Marguerite had reached the age of thirty-three. Then, in 1653, Monsieur Chomedey de Maisonneuve, the governor of the French colony Ville-Marie (present-day Montreal), a saintly man, came to Troyes to visit his sister Louise de Chomedey, who was an Augustinian Canoness. She told him about the prefect of the Marian association, Marguerite Bourgeoys, and suggested that he might be able to recruit her as an educator and teacher for his colony. A meeting came about between Governor Chomedey de Maisonneuve and Marguerite Bourgeoys, who immediately recognized this man as the one who some time previously had been shown to her in an interior vision by God.

After a thorough discussion, Marguerite declared that she was ready to travel with the governor to Ville-Marie in Canada and to open a school there, if her spiritual director agreed to it. Father Gendret, after demanding three days' time to think it over, told her, "Go in peace and entrust yourself to the discretion of this nobleman (Maisonneuve)! He will be the guardian of your purity, for he is a high-ranking knight of the Queen of the Angels." When Marguerite's decision became known, a storm of opposition arose in the city of Troyes and in the vicinity. Even though a Jesuit in Paris, who had been a missionary in Canada, confirmed that she had decided correctly, according to God's will, others urgently tried to dissuade her from her plan.

In the Capuchin church in Nantes, Marguerite complained to the Savior of her interior distress and swore to him that she would seek nothing but his holy will; she asked the Lord for light and counsel. "Then, in an instant," she herself wrote, "all of my interior anguish was transformed; I received the strong impression and a great certainty that I should make this voyage, and I left the church with the firm conviction: God wants me to go to Canada." The Blessed Mother, for her part, gave her the similar assurance: "Go now, I will not forsake you!"

So she went and embarked on July 20, 1653, for Canada; in Ville-Marie, where she arrived on November 16, 1653, in all of the charitable works that she performed, whether as the employee of the governor, as a nurse in the hospital, as a midwife, as a teacher and foundress of a Marian association modeled on the one in

Troyes, again and again she experienced the support of Mary, to whom she was so tenderly devoted. On April 30, 1658, Marguerite Bourgeoys opened the first school in Montreal.

Since she could no longer manage the growing work by herself, she thought of recruiting co-workers from her homeland. For this purpose she voyaged three times to France, amid great difficulties and dangers. On the first voyage she took with her Mademoiselle Mance, the foundress of the hospital in Montreal, who had fallen sick. She was then miraculously healed by that great devotee of Mary, Jean-Jacques Olier (d. 1657), the founder of the Society of Priests of Saint-Sulpice, who had promoted the founding of Montreal in 1642 and then in 1657 had sent the first priests of his Society to the mission there.[2]

On her first voyage to France (1659), Marguerite Bourgeoys found in her hometown, Troyes, four daughters of good families who decided to join her. With these companions she then founded the Congregation of Notre Dame in Montreal. The Sisters strove constantly, in their personal life and in their charitable and educational work, to imitate as perfectly as possible the life of the Blessed Virgin Mary.

In 1675 the bishop of Quebec, Blessed François de Montmorency-Laval, approved the young religious congregation. In composing a rule for the community, Marguerite Bourgeoys was assisted by the Sulpician priest Tronson, who notably stood by her also when the successor of Bishop Montmorency-Laval, Bishop J. de Saint Vallier, caused her great difficulties by his insistence that

[2] One element in the spirituality of Olier and of the Society of Sulpicians, which he founded, is the imitation of the interior life of the Blessed Mother. The principal feast of the Sulpicians is the Presentation of the Blessed Virgin Mary. On this day, year after year, the priests of Saint-Sulpice renew their "vows" and reaffirm their true devotion to Mary, who, according to Olier, is the universal channel of grace and the rich source from which consecrated persons in particular can draw upon the interior life of Christ and make it their own. Marguerite Bourgeoys must have assimilated much of this Marian spirituality of Olier and his Sulpicians on her first voyage to France and even more in the following years, after Louis Tronson, who was Olier's third successor as director of the Society of Saint-Sulpice, became her most trusted counselor.

the Notre Dame congregation be combined with the community of Ursulines that had been transplanted to Canada by Blessed Mary of the Incarnation (Guyart-Martin).

For years many other problems, too, burdened the valiant woman and her foundation, which nevertheless developed very successfully under the wise direction of the blesseds. Despite all these difficulties, Marguerite Bourgeoys, unperturbed, continued bravely on her way, always striving to imitate Mary's virtues.

In the process for beatification it was testified about her: "Mary had already given her special proofs of her benevolence, but Sister Marguerite Bourgeoys kept applying herself to the imitation of her amiable heavenly Instructress, in every way that she could. Unceasingly she kept this consummate example of all perfection before her eyes and urged her companions, also, to imitate the virtues of Mary."

Once, when she was pressured to make her community houses strictly cloistered, she replied from the perspective of her deep Marian spirituality: "Can we ever have a more powerful protector of our consecrated virginity than she, who is the model of God-pleasing purity, whom God destined as his special instrument for the mystery of his Son's Incarnation and who—preserved immaculate and free from original sin—is our principal advocate?"

On January 12, 1700, this brave, humble, and wise woman died in Montreal. Just as once, before she emigrated to Canada, Mary had said to her, "Go, I will not forsake you!", so the Mother of God may have said to her now in the hour of her death: "Come and enter into the joy of your Master! I have never forsaken you, because you have imitated me so faithfully!"

Pope Pius XII beatified Marguerite Bourgeoys on November 12, 1950. Then, on October 31, 1982, Pope John Paul II canonized this great Frenchwoman and on that occasion portrayed the new saint and her beneficial work in Canada as follows:

Her missionary concern attracted [Saint Marguerite Bourgeoys] to the new world of America, and following the footsteps of the holy Canadian martyrs, giving up everything and leaving without baggage and money, she consecrated herself as a lay instructor for the children. This work of being a schoolmistress of the populace she performed with great competence, without making any distinction between the Indian girls and the daughters of the colonists. She esteemed them all as very precious, "as drops of the Blood of Our Lord". She wished to prepare them through a complete education to become good mothers of families. She was concerned to be sure, to form them in the faith, in piety, in a Christian and apostolic way of life, but also to initiate them in the domestic arts and in the practical work which would enable them to subsist on the fruits of their labour, but above all she was concerned to set in order and embellish the home lives of rich and poor.

Decency and intellectual formation were equally on her programme, and the result was that their daughters came forth more literate than their sons, a precursory and rare sign, in [that] epoch, of the authentic advancement of women. She knew how to trust in the capacity of the Indian women, who themselves were not slow in becoming schoolmistresses. One must also note this particular activity: instead of attracting students to boarding-school in the great city... she preferred schools to be situated on the land near the people, ever open to the presence and suggestions of the parents....

Now Marguerite Bourgeoys deemed it no less indispensable to do all in her power to lay the foundations for sound and healthy families. She had then to contribute to the solution of a problem very particular to that place and time. For those men who arrived as soldiers and land-settlers in this new world she knew that there was a lack of worthy spouses [so she should remedy this by establishing] at Ville-Marie a centre of evangelization different from the other colonizations. Marguerite Bourgeoys went in search ... of robust French girls of real virtue. And she watched over them as a mother, with affection and confidence; she received them into her home in order to prepare them to become wives and worthy mothers, Christians, cultured, hard-working, radiant mothers. At the same time, because of her goodness, she helped the rough men become understanding husbands and good fathers.

But she did not stop there. Where *the homes* were founded, she continued to bring them material sustenance on occasions of scarcity and sickness; and she [arranged for the families, especially for the women, opportunities for recreation and fellowship, so that their good resolutions might be strengthened and renewed. She also planned days of recollection and retreats for them to deepen their spirituality].

In brief, what many are trying to do today, with methods, institutions and associations suitable for our times, for a first-class education, for a preparation for Christian marriage, for the work of counselling and sustaining homes, appears to be found in germ, under other methods, in the spirit and initiatives of Marguerite Bourgeoys. . . .

And let us not forget that Marguerite was sustained in her astonishing work by her devotion to the Holy Family and that in the midst of the greatest difficulties—"sorrows and fatigues"— she served the families with the quality of love which comes from the Holy Spirit.[3]

---

[3] "Two Authentic Responses to the Call of Love", *L'Osservatore romano*, November 8, 1982, pp. 1–2.

Saint
Jeanne Delanoue

Foundress

b. June 18, 1660, Saumur (France)
d. August 17, 1736, Saumur

Canonized October 31, 1982

Jeanne Delanoue,[1] who was beatified on November 9, 1947, and canonized on October 31, 1982, together with Blessed Marguerite Bourgeoys, was born on June 18, 1660, in the French city of Saumur as the twelfth of twelve children of a modest shopkeeper. During her childhood and youth she experienced religious fervor at times, which alternated with periods of indifference and lukewarmness; for the time being she followed her father's example and worked as a shrewd businesswoman.

Then one day she happened to meet the saintly Madame Françoise Souchet in Rennes, who revealed her true vocation to her, namely, to care for the poor and to give an example of heroic love of neighbor.

Despite opposition from several sides, including that of her confessor, she opened a home for orphans in 1700. So as to be able to care for them properly and educate them, from 1703 on she recruited other women to assist her. This soon developed into a

---

[1] F. Trochu, *La Bienheureuse Jeanne Delanoue: Soeur Jeanne de la Croix, fondatrice des soeurs de S. Anne de la Providence de Saumur* (Lyons, 1938).

religious association. On the feast of Saint Anne, July 26, 1704, the first Sisters of the Congregation of Saint Anne of Providence received the habit. On September 24, 1709, the newly formed congregation was recognized and approved by the bishop of Angers, and Jeanne Delanoue, who now took the name Mother Jeanne of the Cross, was designated the superior. By 1727 this religious congregation had matured to the point where it numbered twenty-four Sisters, who devoted themselves to caring for approximately three hundred orphans and elderly people in need.

Problems soon cropped up in the community as a result of Jansenist influences. Mother Jeanne of the Cross, however, pointed her little community down the path of sound doctrine, especially with regard to the reception of Holy Communion. On the basis of her personal gift for the discernment of spirits, she made great progress in the spiritual life, and God granted her various extraordinary favors, such as ecstasies and visions.

On August 17, 1736, Mother Jeanne of the Cross died at the age of seventy-six, having gained great merit through the countless works of charity that she had performed personally and through the Sisters of her congregation. Pope John Paul II aptly characterized this saint of charity in his homily at the solemn ceremony of canonization in Saint Peter's in Rome on October 31, 1982, as follows:

Saint Jeanne Delanoue, the last of twelve children, . . . came to the help of families . . . in the context of her town of Saumur at the end of the seventeenth century, which was marked with great material and social difficulties, aggravated by famines, bad harvests and severe winters. One recalls above all her efficacious help for the poorest of the poor. She who was known above all as a wise and shrewd trader, became suddenly "a very great prodigy of charity", when the Holy Spirit, extinguishing "the fire of her avarice", made her understand that her ardent faith required also "the fire of that charity" by making her appreciate poverty. The Book of Isaiah tells us at once: "Share your bread with the hungry, receive into your homes the unfortunate who have no shelter, clothe those without clothing, do not steal from your fellow man".

This is what Jeanne Delanoue carried out to the letter. She visited those who lived like animals in stables dug into the hills; she brought them food and clothing; she washed their clothes and gave them whatever they needed; she undertook to heat these precarious shelters; she gave generously to those who passed by; she began to take them into her own lodgings, then she successively furnished three houses which were given to her and which she named "Providences", so that she could receive there orphan children, young girls left to themselves, women in distress, old and indigent people of all kinds, suffering from hunger and cold, in short, all those who would say to her on the judgment day: I was hungry, thirsty, I was naked, sick, without a shelter. She did not like to make any distinction between the poor who merited her service and those who did not. She came to the aid of all, but she also wished to help them work, to teach a trade to the children and the young girls.

Still more, Jeanne Delanoue experienced the humiliations of the poor, even venturing at times to beg, taking for herself food often worse than theirs, without taking account of her continual fasting, her short and uncomfortable nights. She wished her sisters to share the same home as the poor, eating as they did, being treated as they were in cases of sickness, and dressed in a humble grey habit. As for the poor, she knew how to surround them with tenderness, at times procuring for them festive meals, requiring that her sisters treat them with respect and serve them before themselves.

The townspeople, even the priests, criticized her "excessive" austerities and her "disordered" charities. But nothing stopped her, not even the failure of her first [hospice]: "I wish to live and die with my dear brethren, the poor".

Some other undertakings, like those which were born from the charity of St. Vincent de Paul, were already widespread in

France. But at that time Saumur did not even have a hospital, and Jeanne Delanoue wanted to create a great service of charity for the indigent and the sick abandoned to themselves. She wished to organize visits to them and eventually to open small schools for their children. In her time, with the means at her disposal, she learned how to remedy poverty and vagrancy. Her example will not fail to challenge our modern world. So many countries live in dire poverty! And even the industrialized nations do not escape material anxieties; they have their poor of all sorts. Today one may perhaps strive with greater advantage to discover the causes of these miseries, and to create more just conditions for all and to establish measures of foresight, so as to help the poor to help themselves without leaving them to be merely assisted. But the care for the indigent, the love of the poor, immediate and efficacious help will always remain fundamental to remedy the harshness of our modern world. It is at this price, says Isaiah, "that the light will arise in the darkness".

Finally, when we proclaim the holiness of Jeanne Delanoue, it is important to try to understand the *spiritual secret* of her peerless dedication. It does seem that her temperament led her to an interest in the poor through sentimentality or pity. But the Holy Spirit himself led her to see *Christ* in the poor, the Christ-Child in their children—she had a particular devotion to him—Christ the friend of the poor, Christ himself, humiliated and crucified. And with Christ she wished to show to the poor the tenderness of the Father. To this God she had recourse with the audacity of a child, expecting everything from him, from his Providence, the name with which she designated her homes and her foundation from their very origin: the Congregation of St. Anne of Providence. Her constant devotion to Mary was inseparable from that of the Blessed Trinity. The Eucharistic mystery was also at the heart of her life. All this was very far from the prevailing Jansenism. Her attachment to the Church dissuaded her from taking new ways without consulting her confessors and the bishop of the diocese. . . .

Jeanne Delanoue attained very quickly not only the heroism of virtues, the evangelical virtues of the Sermon on the Mount, but also a profound contemplation of the divine persons with mystical signs of the highest union with God according to the unitive way, exceptionally inflamed with love for Jesus, "her Spouse". That was the source of the inspiration and achievement of the "folly" of her charity and of the boldness of her undertakings. May the Church of today beware of forgetting this: as at the end of the seventeenth century and the beginning of the eighteenth, there will be no true reform today nor any fruitful movements without *an authentic mystical current*.[2]

[2] "Two Authentic Responses to the Call of Love", *L'Osservatore romano*, November 8, 1982, pp. 2, 12.

Saint
Leopold Mandić

Capuchin, Confessor

*b. May 12, 1866, Castelnuovo
(near Cattarvo, Dalmatia)*
d. July 30, 1942, Padua

Canonized October 16, 1983

This saintly Capuchin,[1] who for decades in Padua was an extraordinarily dedicated apostle of reconciliation by means of the Sacrament of Divine Mercy, was born on May 12, 1866, in Castelnuovo, near Cattarvo in Dalmatia, as the last of twelve children of the Croatian couple Mandić-Zarevic. At his baptism he received the Croatian name Bogdan (i.e., Theodore: gift from God). He was blessed with a solid religious education provided by his parents at home. To all outward appearances there was nothing about him that suggested future greatness—the boy was dwarfish (four feet six inches) and somewhat deformed; he had, moreover, a very weak voice and spoke with a lisp. It was a different story, however, if one considered his intellectual and spiritual aptitude, for he was extremely gifted.

In 1882 the youth entered the Seraphic Minor Seminary of the Capuchins in Udine. Here he heard the call to religious life and so was able to begin the novitiate in 1884 with the Capuchins in

[1] Dr. Lisl Gutwenger, *Pater Leopold Mandic: Der Heilige zwischen Ost und West: Ein charismatischer Beichtvater* (Stein am Rhein: Christiana-Verlag, 1983).

Bassano del Grappa. With the habit he received the religious name Leopold. In 1888 Brother Leopold made his solemn religious profession in Padua. After completing his theology studies in Udine, he was ordained a priest on September 20, 1890, in the church of Santa Maria della Salute in Venice.

The young Capuchin priest then worked from 1890 until 1897 in the Capuchin friary in Venice as a confessor and after that as superior, from 1897 to 1900, in the Capuchin friary at Zara in Dalmatia. After rather short stays in Bassano del Grappa, in Capodistria, and in Thiene, near Vicenza, Father Leopold went to the Capuchin friary in Padua in 1909. Here he remained almost uninterruptedly until his death on July 30, 1942, and for more than thirty years he had his "headquarters"—as he himself put it—in a tiny room annexed between the church and the cloister, a cell without ventilation or sunlight, which was ice-cold in the winter and hot and humid in the summer. Father Leopold sat there for many hours each day in a worn-out armchair so as to bring peace of soul to thousands upon thousands. Hearing confessions for hours on end was practically his only priestly duty for more than thirty years. He had a unique charism for it: in the course of those years thousands of laypeople and numerous priests and bishops—among them one who would later become Pope John Paul I—were instructed and converted, strengthened, consoled, and directed by this wise, enlightened, and kindly confessor. Often they would wait for hours outside Father Leopold's confessional in order to kneel down with confidence at the feet of this little Capuchin priest, to hear his word of forgiveness and to receive his sound advice and his spiritual direction for the future.

God rewarded the apostolic efforts of Father Leopold Mandić in the confessional with quite a few miracles, which he worked even during his lifetime. Almost daily extraordinary things occurred all around him and through him, but everything remained quiet, without attracting attention, as he had prayed God that it might be. Father Leopold could also see prophetically. For instance, years before the actual event, he predicted to a trusted friend the bombing of the

Capuchin friary in Padua in these words: "This cloister and the church will be hit (by the bombs), too, but this cell (his confession room) will not be hit. God has shown so much mercy to souls here; this cell must remain standing as a monument to God's goodness." An air attack on Padua on May 19, 1944, destroyed many houses, and the five large-caliber, high-explosive bombs also reduced the cloister and the church of the Capuchins to rubble and ruins. In the midst of all the ruins the confession room of Father Leopold and a statue of the Blessed Mother remained completely intact.

How did this little Capuchin attract so many people? It was surely the remarkable pastoral wisdom of this father confessor, who was thoroughly educated in theology; then, of course, his unusual knowledge of the human heart and his own good-heartedness, which gave him a great understanding of human weakness. A particularly prominent trait in him, furthermore, was his maternal capacity for sympathy, which he had gained through his great love for and devotion to his heavenly Mother Mary.

Father Leopold's love for Mary supported him in all the troubles of life and endowed him with light for his mind, strength for his heart, kindness and generosity for his soul. The biographer of this saint, who was also his postulator during the beatification and canonization process, Father Pietro Bernardi, O.F.M.Cap., explained: "It is almost impossible to say how much Father Leopold loved the Madonna. The tone of his voice when he spoke of her, the light in his eyes when he looked at a picture of her, cannot be put into words at all. You would have to have seen him in order to comprehend something of the ardent love for Mary in the heart of this Capuchin." Father Leopold's mother before him had been filled with a great love for Mary. Because of this she consecrated her twelfth child very early on to the Mother of God and kindled in his heart that spark that would soon become a blazing fire. Once Father Leopold himself admitted: "Already as a little child I was consecrated to the Mother of God. She awakened in me a vocation to the priesthood and to the religious life, and then preserved and protected it."

Since Father Leopold was by nature a very thoughtful and logical man, he based his Marian devotion, not on mere sentiments, but on a recognition of Mary's greatness in the light of faith. It is remarkable that, of all his theological studies during his entire priestly life, Mariology was his favorite subject. As a young seminarian he had already chosen the book of Father Jean-Nicolas Grou, S.J. (d. 1803), on *The Interior Life of Jesus and Mary* as his preferred reading. He meditated upon it again and again and asked his fellow students to explain whenever he thought he had not understood something as well as he might. In the course of his theology studies he also researched scientific treatises about the Mother of God. He thereby provided himself with a thorough education in the field of Mariology. With a pious passion he studied all the Marian passages in Sacred Scripture, interpreted their meaning, and selected from them the material for his meditations. He could show great displeasure about exegeses that did not do justice to Mary's exalted greatness. Often he would ask his confreres about the views of the Doctors of the Church on the greatness and the privileges of Mary. How he lamented the fact that those two great Doctors of the Church, Bonaventure and Thomas Aquinas, had not grasped clearly and defended the dogma of the Immaculate Conception. When the Venetian province of the Capuchin order published the first volume of the works of Saint Lawrence of Brindisi, his *Mariale*, Father Leopold experienced indescribable joy. He read the book right away and spoke enthusiastically about this work, in which the holy Capuchin Doctor of the Church had glorified the Mother of God so fittingly.

Throughout his life, Father Leopold Mandić had a desire to write a book about Mary as the helpmate of the Redeemer who obtains grace for the faithful. He wanted in this way to help adorn the Blessed Mother with a new diadem: Mary, Mediatrix of All Graces. The constant work in the confessional prevented him from realizing his plan. Out of love for Mary, Father Leopold wanted to render her every conceivable honor. In his confession room he honored an image of Mary and decorated it each day with fresh flowers as an expression of his enduring love for the Most Blessed Virgin. He liked to celebrate Mass in church at the altar dedicated to Mary, and on Saturdays, whenever the rubrics permitted it, he would celebrate the votive Mass of the Immaculate Conception. Every day he prayed, in addition to his breviary, the Little Office of the Blessed Virgin and several Rosaries.

On account of his poor health, his religious superiors forbade him to participate in the monastic prayers at midnight, but on the vigils of Marian feast days he had permission to do so. On such days he increased his prayers and sacrifices in honor of the Mother of God.

His doctor had prescribed that he take regular walks outside the cloister, so on his excursions he would always visit first the nearby parish church of Santa Croce and pray before the picture of the Madonna della Salute. Every Sunday and feast day he would go in the early afternoon hours to the basilica of Santa Giustina, in Padua, to pay his respects to the miraculous image of Our Lady of Constantinople, which the people attributed to Saint Luke the Evangelist.

It often happened, while Father Leopold was hearing confessions or conversing with someone, that he would suddenly excuse himself and hurry off to church for a moment, to the altar of our Lady. Then he would return, radiant with joy.

Father Leopold loved the Blessed Mother, and his confidence in her power and goodness was unshakeable. That is why he often advised his penitents in their troubles and concerns: "Turn to the Blessed Virgin! After all, we know from our faith that she is the great patroness to whom all must have recourse."

Father Leopold saw the salvation of the human race in the Mother of God. She preserves mankind from the ruin that it has merited by its sins. One of Father Leopold's sayings was: "If the Immaculate Virgin does not rescue us, then we are already lost. If she does not intercede for us with her Son, then the mercy of God cannot take the place of his justice."

This unlimited trust in Mary was based on Father Leopold's

conviction that the Blessed Mother cannot forsake us, her children, for whom she suffered so much under the Cross of Christ. Once he wrote, "Through the Immaculate we received in Jesus, the adorable fruit of her womb, the life of grace. Mary mysteriously gave us birth to this new life under the Cross through the most bitter martyrdom that a mother's heart has ever suffered. We are truly the children of her tears and pains."

Father Leopold urged all those who were suffering to take refuge in Mary with confidence that they would not be rejected.

Whenever he spoke, Father Leopold never ceased recommending love and devotion to the Blessed Virgin. Again and again he talked to his penitents about the Mother of God. He often asked the priests who came to him for confession whether and how they proclaimed Mary's greatness and glories to the faithful in their sermons. A Third Order Franciscan from Padua wrote, "I remember the repeated admonition of Father Leopold: 'Honor the Mother of God! She can do everything. She is our Mother!' Then he would add, ardently and urgently, 'O, the Madonna! The Madonna!' With this constant invocation of Mary he seemed to commend the souls kneeling before him to the Blessed Virgin. I seemed to be transformed merely by these words of Father Leopold. I felt how the Blessed Mother, through this exclamation of Father Leopold, had understood the needs of my soul. Father Leopold, that pure and humble religious, led souls safely to the Mother of God!"

During his assignment at the friary in Thiene, near Vicenza, in the years 1906 to 1909, Father Leopold often helped the lay brothers humbly with the household chores, washed the dishes, cleaned the cells, and set the table. Since his soul was turned constantly toward God, he wanted them to pray during their work, especially the Litany of Loreto. At the invocation "Cause of our joy", he interrupted his work, lifted his eyes to heaven, and remained for a while in this attitude, as though enraptured. Once a confrere asked him, "Father Leopold, why do you interrupt your work at this invocation of the Litany of Loreto and raise your eyes to heaven?" At that he exclaimed, "O Madonna, the Madonna, the cause of our joy!" Then he remained looking up to heaven for a long time, his face beaming.

This tender, childlike, confident love of Father Leopold for the Mother of God could seem to be an astonishing phenomenon to someone who did not know his interior dispositions. Toward Mary he had the same attitude as that of an innocent child to his mother. He arrived at such a childlike trust in Mary because in the spiritual anguish that quite often burdened and oppressed him, and in his concern for his penitents, he would always take refuge in the Blessed Mother.

Without a doubt, Mary responded to such a loving devotion with great kindness and generosity. Even during Father Leopold's lifetime, prayers were answered miraculously when he brought to Mary the troubles and concerns of particular persons in their need. As for him, Mary stood by him at all times, consoled him during the terrible spiritual trials, restored peace to his tortured soul, strengthened him in his physical sufferings, and helped him to give fresh courage to the sinners and unfortunates who came to him and to lead them back to the right path.

In July 1934 Father Leopold had the opportunity to take part in a pilgrimage to Lourdes. For years he had longed to visit that fountain of graces that had been sanctified by the appearances of the immaculately conceived Mother of God. A number of his penitents invited Father Leopold to be the chaplain for their trip and paid for his travel expenses. During the journey he continually made the rounds in the infirmary cars of the train, because all the people wanted to make their confessions to him.

In Lourdes itself Father Leopold experienced almost heavenly joys; he became completely absorbed in praying and hearing confessions. As he celebrated Holy Mass at the altar in the grotto of the apparitions in Lourdes, he received through our Lady's intercession utterly extraordinary graces and supernatural illuminations, which only a soul already far advanced along the path to perfection and sanctity could understand. During the grand religious demonstrations in Lourdes, Father Leopold took part in the procession of lights and the procession of the Blessed Sacrament with such fervent faith that all who were near him were edified to an uncommon degree. With his face radiant he exclaimed, "We have seen marvelous things here!"

On the trip back to Padua, Father Leopold, through Mary's intercession, just missed a traffic accident that might have been fatal. "It was the Madonna who rescued us!" he cried when he arrived home. In this, as in numerous instances, the Blessed Mother showed that she was pleased with this humble priest, who had such a childlike trust in her and who often reaffirmed it by saying, "I expect everything from the powerful intercession of our Lady, from her maternal heart!"

The little Capuchin priest Leopold Mandić, who was so great in his self-sacrificial zeal for souls, was beatified on May 2, 1976, by Pope Paul VI; after a very short time, on the basis of a new miracle worked through his intercession, he was canonized on October 16, 1983, by Pope John Paul II. Perhaps the lessons that this new saint would like to and ought to teach us are (1) that priests should again become more zealous in administering the Sacrament of Reconciliation, and (2) that everyone, priests and lay faithful alike, should regain a great esteem for this undervalued and neglected Sacrament of the Mercy of God, and also (3) that we should have a childlike confidence in the Mother of God, Refuge of Sinners.

Father Leopold was canonized precisely on the fifth anniversary of the election of Cardinal Karol Wojtyla as the Successor of Peter. Pope John Paul II, during his trip to Padua, visited also the grave of Father Leopold, prayed there, and then sat on the old, rickety chair in which Father Leopold used to sit for hours while hearing confessions. It was as though the Pope were saying to priests: Prize well this power to forgive sins, which was conferred on you at your ordination, as highly as Father Leopold did, and make zealous use of it in the confessional! And when you do, have also, like Father Leopold, a very great confidence in the Mother of God, the Refuge of Sinners, who at Fatima so strongly recommended and requested prayers for the conversion of sinners.

Father Leopold, until the final moment of his life, placed his complete trust in his heavenly Mother. When he died, on July 30, 1942, his last words were the conclusion of the Salve Regina: "O tender, O loving, O sweet Virgin Mary!"

Here now are excerpts from the homily Pope John Paul II gave on October 16, 1983, during the solemn canonization of Father Leopold Mandić in Saint Peter's Square in Rome:

Leopold Mandić . . . , a heroic servant of reconciliation and penance . . . , [was] born in Castelnovo near Cattaro. He left his family and homeland at the age of sixteen to enter the Capuchin seminary in Udine. His was a largely uneventful life: some changes from one convent to another, as is customary with the Capuchins, but nothing more. Then came his assignment to the convent in Padua, where he remained until his death.

Well, precisely into this poverty of a life that was externally irrelevant, the Holy Spirit came and enkindled a new grandeur: a heroic fidelity to Christ, to the Franciscan ideal, and to priestly service towards his brothers and sisters.

Saint Leopold did not leave us any theological or literary works, he did not attract people with his culture, he did not found any social works. To all those who knew him, he was nothing but a poor friar, small and sickly.

His greatness lay elsewhere: *in immolating himself*, in giving himself, day after day, for the entire span of his priestly life, for fifty-two years, in the silence, in the reserve, in the *humility of a confession room*: "the good shepherd lays down his life for his sheep". Father Leopold was always there, ready and smiling, prudent and modest, the discreet confidant and faithful father of souls, a respectful teacher and an understanding and patient spiritual adviser.

If we would want to describe him with a single word, as his penitents and confreres did during his life, then he is "the confessor": he knew only how "to hear confessions". And it \is precisely here that his greatness lies: in his fading into the background to give place to the true Shepherd of souls. He expressed his commitment in this way: "We hide everything, even what may appear to be a gift of God, so as not to make it an instrument of profit. To God alone be honour and glory! If it were possible, we should pass over the earth like a shadow that leaves no trace." And to whoever asked him how he could live that way, he would answer, "It is my life!"

"The good shepherd lays down his life for his sheep." To the human eye, our saint's life seems like a tree, all of whose branches an invisible and cruel hand has lopped off one by one. Father Leopold was a priest for whom preaching was impossible because of a speech defect. He was a priest who ardently wanted to dedicate himself to the missions, and up to the very end he was awaiting the day of departure, but never left because his health was so frail. He was a priest who had such a great ecumenical spirit that he offered himself as a victim to the Lord, with a daily self-giving, that full unity might be reestablished between the Latin Church and the still separated Oriental Churches, and that there might be "one flock under one shepherd" (cf. Jn 10:16); but he lived his ecumenical vocation in a totally hidden way. Weeping, he confided: "I will be a missionary here, in obedience and in the exercise of my ministry". And again: "Every soul who seeks my ministry will meanwhile be my Orient".

What remained for Saint Leopold? For whom and for what did his life serve? Brothers and sisters who had lost God, love and hope remained for him. Poor human beings who needed God and invoked him, pleading for his forgiveness, his consolation, his peace, his serenity. To these "poor", Saint Leopold gave his life; for them he offered his sorrows and his prayer; but above all, with them he celebrated the Sacrament of Reconciliation. It is here that he lived out his charism. He celebrated the Sacrament of Reconciliation, exercising his ministry in the shadow of the Crucified Christ. His glance was fixed on the crucifix that hung over the penitent's kneeler. The Crucified was always the main character. "It is he who pardons, it is he who absolves!" He, the Shepherd of the flock.

Saint Leopold immersed his ministry in prayer and contemplation. He was a confessor of continual prayer, a confessor who habitually lived absorbed in God, in a supernatural atmosphere. . . .

The Church, in placing before us today the figure of her humble servant Saint Leopold, who guided so many souls, wants also to point out these *hands that are raised to heaven* during the various struggles of man and of the People of God.

They are raised in prayer. And they are raised in the gesture of absolving sins, which *always reaches that love* which is God: that love which once for all was revealed to us in the Crucified and Risen Christ. . . .

Dear brothers, what do Moses' hands, raised in prayer, say to us? What do the hands of Saint Leopold, the humble servant of the confessional, say to us? They tell us that the Church can never tire of giving witness to God who is love![2]

[2] "Saintly Hero of the Confessional", *L'Osservatore romano*, October 24, 1983, pp. 1, 3.

INDEX OF SAINTS AND BLESSEDS